GALATEO

or,

THE RULES OF
Polite Behavior

Conciosia cosa, che tu mecominci pur hora quel uiaggio,
del quale io ho la maggior parte, si come tu uedi, fornito;
cioe questa uita mortale, auendo io assai, come io fo, ho
proposto meco di uenirti moshando quando un luogo et qua
do una leua, doue io, si come quello che gli ho sperimentati;
temo, che tu caminando per essa, potresti ageuolmente o cadere
o errare; accioche tu ammaestrato da me possa tenere la diritta
uia con salute dell'anima tua et con laude et honore della
uostra honoreuole et nobile famiglia; et percio che la tua tenera
eta non sarebbe sufficiente a riceuere piu principali et piu
sottili ammaestramenti, riserbando quegli a piu conueneuol
tempo, incomincero da quello, che per auentura potrebbe
a molti parer frixolo, cio e quello, che io stimo che ti con
uenga di fare per potere in comunicando et in usando con
le genti essere costumato et piaceuole et di bella maniera:
il che non di meno e o uirtu o cosa molto a uirtu simigliante;
et come che, lo essere liberale o costante o magnanimo sia per
se stessa alcun fatto piu laudabil cosa et maggiore, che non
e l'essere aueneuole et costumato, non dimeno forse che la
dolcezza de costumi et la conueneuolezza de modi et delle
maniere et delle parole giouano non meno a i possessori d'esse
che la grandezza dell'animo et la sicurezza altrui a
loro possessori non fanno: pereio che quelle si conuengono
exercitare ogni di molte uolte conciosia che a ciascuno e
necessario di usare con gli altri huomini ogni di et di fauel
lare ogni di con essoloro ma la giustitia la fortezza le
altre uirtu piu nobili et maggiori si pongano in opera piu di rado

GALATEO

or,

THE RULES OF
Polite Behavior

GIOVANNI DELLA CASA

Edited and Translated by M. F. Rusnak

The University of Chicago Press
Chicago and London

The University of Chicago Press, Chicago 60637
The University of Chicago Press, Ltd., London
© 2013 by The University of Chicago
All rights reserved. Published 2013.
Paperback edition 2014
Printed in the United States of America

23 22 21 20 19 18 17 16 15 14   4 5 6 7 8

ISBN-13: 978-0-226-01097-7 (cloth)
ISBN-13: 978-0-226-21219-7 (paperback)
ISBN-13: 978-0-226-01102-8 (e-book)
DOI: 10.7208/chicago/9780226011028.001.0001

Frontispiece: First page of *Galateo* (Vat. Lat. 14825,
c. 45r.). The original, unexpurgated version is at
present the only contemporary manuscript version.
Photograph © Biblioteca Apostolica Vaticana.

Library of Congress Cataloging in Publication Data

Della Casa, Giovanni, 1503–1556.
Galateo, or, The rules of polite behavior /
Giovanni Della Casa ; edited and translated by
M. F. Rusnak.
    pages.   cm.
Includes bibliographical references.
ISBN 978-0-226-01097-7 (cloth : alk paper) —
ISBN 978-0-226-01102-8 (e-book) 1. Etiquette,
Medieval—Early works to 1800. 2. Conversation—
Early works to 1800. I. Rusnak, M. F. II. Title. III.
Title: Rules of polite behavior.
BJ1921.D4413 2013
395—dc23   2013005588

♾ This paper meets the requirements of ANSI/NISO
Z39.48-1992 (Permanence of Paper).

Contents

TRATTATO
DI MESER GIOVANNI
*della casa, nel quale sotto la persona d'un uecchio
idiota ammaestrante un suo giouanetto si ra-
giona de modi, che si debbono ò tenere, ò
schifare nella comune conuersatione,
cognominato Galatheo.*

IN MILANO
Appresso à Giouann'Antonio de gli Antonij.
M D L I X.

Title page from the Milanese edition of *Galateo* (1559), the first
separate publication. Photograph courtesy of the Beinecke Rare Book
and Manuscript Library, Yale University.

Introduction

In *Della nobiltà di dame* (Venice, 1600), dancing master Fabritio Caroso tells us that women, when walking, should take great care never to give the impression that their feet are more than three fingers off the ground. By placing the foot firmly and straightening the knee attentively, the lady would be able to move ahead "with all grace, decorum, and beauty."[1] This is the world of Giovanni Della Casa's *Galateo* (1558), the great Renaissance guidebook for anyone who wants to look attractive and not give offense. It is one of the two or three treatises of the Renaissance that taught good manners to the whole of Europe, as Arnaldo Di Benedetto, a contemporary critic and editor of Della Casa's writings, describes it. Another critic, J. E. Spingarn, considered one of the great public intellectuals of the early twentieth century, put it this way: "Many books had touched the subject on one or more of its sides, but no single book had attempted to formulate the whole code of refined conduct for their time and indeed for all time."[2]

Taking the form of a brief and readable guide to everyday courtesy, what we should do and, even more important, what we should not do, *Galateo* has much in common with two better-known manuals of the Italian Renaissance: Castiglione's *Book of the Courtier* (1528) and Machiavelli's *The Prince* (1532). *Galateo* is to etiquette what *The Prince* is to politics, a discourse on action in real life based on the study of the classics and close observation of a complex world. Unlike Castiglione, who wrote from within the Ducal Palace of Urbino, Della Casa does not address the *sprezzatura* (nonchalance) of idealized courtiers in fancy black dress. Instead, his recommendations are directed toward anyone who has a social life.

On the most basic level, then, *Galateo* is a collection of precepts on how we should behave in public places, where we are on public view. Although the author was the archbishop of Benevento, he is not interested in the bigger questions of virtue and vice. Instead, he turns his close attention to what that master of propriety Samuel Johnson called "the minuter decencies and inferior duties." By dramatizing the trivial behavior of his contemporaries, Della Casa sought "to regulate the practice of daily conversation, to correct those depravities which are rather ridiculous than criminal, and remove those grievances which, if they produce no lasting calamities, impress hourly vexation." Della Casa, writing at the end of a long career in the public eye, wanted to get down in writing what it means to be civilized.

What makes Della Casa's approach so arresting is the intensity with which he examines our smallest gestures and daily acts. As he writes, "And don't be looking like you consider the things discussed above trivial and of small moment, for even light blows, if they are many, can kill" (chap. 3).

WHO WAS GALATEO?

Giovanni Della Casa (1503–56) was born to a wealthy family from the area above Florence called Mugello, the same countryside where Lorenzo de' Medici went hunting and stayed at the Villa Cafaggiolo. Although Della Casa always regarded himself as Florentine, his life was spent mostly outside of Florence. As he notes in the opening lines of *Galateo*, he was constantly on the move throughout Italy: Bologna, Padua, Rome, Venice, and Treviso.

His early education, which began in Rome where his father was staying on business, was exceptional and based on Latin and Greek classics. The first of his several tutors was Ubaldino Bandinelli, a distinguished humanist whom he recalls in *Galateo*. He moved to Bologna to study jurisprudence but was drawn away, much as Petrarch was, by the lure of manuscripts and ancient literature. In his early twenties, Della Casa spent a year studying at his family home with Ludovico Beccadelli, another outstanding scholar of Aristotle and Cicero. He then transferred to Padua, where he befriended the accomplished linguist Pietro Bembo, some thirty years his senior and one of the most powerful intellects of the time. As Della Casa's brief biography of Bembo (with its touches of autobiography) makes clear, nothing had greater literary prestige at the time than mastering Greek, Latin, and Tuscan. It was in Florence, Della Casa writes, that Bembo's "tender ears and spirit drank of that pure and sweet Tuscan language." Bembo's early writings in Latin and in Italian were remarkable: "there was nothing . . . more refined, more elegant, or more *soave* to hear."[3]

By the early 1530s, Della Casa had decided to pursue an ecclesiastic career at the Vatican, and he was nominated archbishop of Benevento in 1544. He was following a prestigious career path, suitable for someone with his literary and linguistic gifts, and his writing (mostly in Latin) during this time took the form of orations and letters, often involving

The ancestral Della Casa family villa in Borgo San Lorenzo, Tuscany.
Photograph by Adriano Gasparrini.

quite delicate international affairs. Only in the last five years of his life did Della Casa return to writing poetry and literary prose, secluded in the rural outskirts of Treviso, retired and apparently detached from church affairs. In search of *oblio* (a scholarly retreat from worldly concerns), he went to the abbey at Nervesa near Treviso, which was bombed in World War I to become the suggestive ruin it is today. *Galateo* was first published in 1558, two years after he died.

The title is simply the first name in Latin of another friend and teacher: Galeazzo Florimonte (1478–1567). Florimonte was the bishop of Sessa Aurunca (near Naples); he was famous in Italy at the time and the author of a commentary on Aristotle's *Ethics*. Florimonte encouraged Della Casa to write an etiquette book, having himself attempted something similar. From all accounts, Florimonte appears to have been a model of refined behavior, self-control, and literary erudition. One of four judges on the Council of Trent, Florimonte was, according to the editor of the first edition of *Galateo*, "admired for his doctrine, and for his manners, and for the goodness and sincerity of his nature, and for true Christian piety and the highest religious faith."

Giovanni Della Casa was well prepared to record his thoughts on the subject of good living. Spingarn puts it well: "As a scion of two distinguished Florentine families (his mother was a Tornabuoni), as an eminent prelate and diplomatist, an accomplished poet and orator, a master of Tuscan prose, a frequenter of all the fashionable circles of his day, the author of licentious capitoli, and more especially as one whose morals were distinctly not above reproach, he seemed eminently fitted for the office of arbiter elegantiarum."[4] Della Casa also had the advantage of having a specific audience in mind, which never hurts an author. *Galateo* was likely addressed to his nephew Annibale, the son of Della Casa's sister, Dianora, and Luigi Rucellai, a member of the ancient and powerful Florentine Rucellai family. Giovanni Rucellai (1475–1525) was the head of the household, a gifted classicist who commissioned many great artworks of the Florentine Renaissance, including Leon Battista Alberti's Palazzo Rucellai and the great façade of the Church of Santa Maria Novella. Della Casa's letters suggest that he was particularly attached to Annibale, who must have been a boy or young man at the time *Galateo* was composed, as his death is documented in 1601. This biography gives a poignancy to a line in *Galateo*: "If those who took care of me in childhood, when we are tender and impressionable, had known how to bend my habits, maybe somewhat hard and coarse by nature, and how to soften and polish them, I could probably have become the man I am now trying to make of you" (chap. 25).

Giovanni Della Casa is buried in the Church of Sant'Andrea delle Valle in Rome.

THE HISTORY OF / IN CONDUCT BOOKS

Della Casa lived in Florence and Rome at the same time as Michelangelo. While the Florentine Renaissance is usually associated with works of visual art and architecture, such as the iconic David or Leonardo da Vinci's famous "Vitruvian Man," there were writers equally focused on defining the ideal. It is within the Italian Renaissance courts and cities that writers first began to reflect on and record the characteristics of the ideal courtier and sophisticated behavior not bound to the spiritual and chivalric codes of the medieval period.

Proper conduct was considered an art as demanding and rewarding as ceramics or jewelry making. Italian humanists like Galeazzo Florimonte examined the rules of proper behavior, influenced by careful study of Aristotle and Plato. As Rudolph Bell writes in *How to Do It: Guides to Good Living for Renaissance Italians,* with works like Speroni Speroni's *I dialogi* (1542), Giovambattista Nenna of Bari's *Il Nennio* (1542), Girolomo Muzio's *Il gentilhuomo* (1571), Torquato Tasso's *Il forno* (1580), and Annibale Romei's *Discorsi* (1585), Italians of the Renaissance created a new way of looking at human conduct. "Eagerly consumed by Italy's urban nobility," Bell writes, "translations brought the new civility to France, England, Spain, and eventually even to the uncouth Germans."[5] So much was Italy associated with decency and decorum by the time of Shakespeare that some among the English were ridiculed for vainly following the Italian trend, "since *Galateo* came in, and Tuscanisme gan usurpe."[6]

In a fine study of the subject, Anna Bryson notes that England was still too rural to develop rules of civility, and so there developed a "craze for Italian courtliness."

Much of the history of how people behaved in private life and the changing codes of conduct is still being written. *Galateo* is an important source for how people conducted themselves and is the font of all later etiquette books; Spingarn even considers Della Casa the Euclid of etiquette. Other scholars have shown interest in *Galateo,* and they have traced the complex circulation of ideas on conduct in the early modern period from Domenico Mancini's *De quatuor virtutibus* (1523) to Henry Peachum's *The Compleat Gentleman* (1622) and Richard Brathwaite's *The English Gentleman* (1630). These texts have been often segregated, however, into the restricted genre of "conduct books," treated as niche literature, far inferior to the drama or the music of the time.

Historians have also used *Galateo* effectively to explore complex historical and political issues of the period. *Galateo* has been used, for instance, as a starting point to talk about the Counter-Reformation, the Council of Trent, and the 1549 *Index of Prohibited Books.* As papal nuncio (that is, official Vatican representative) to Venice, Della Casa was active in all these seminal events, during one of the most turbulent periods in the history of Italy and the Roman church.[7]

A MODEL OF TUSCAN LITERATURE

The risk of either historical approach to Galateo is overlooking its value as literature. With its vibrant colloquial language, allusions to classical literature and proverbs, and anecodotes and turns of phrase, *Galateo* is literature of the first rank. Della Casa was celebrated in Italy for the book's purity and elegance. The poet Giacomo Leopardi believed that Della Casa wrote in the finest Attic style, that is, the refined clear prose writing associated with ancient Greece. "If you would hear . . . the voices of Plato and Aristotle and Cicero, and of many others with your ears purged, you would know that all other glories are vain," Della Casa wrote in a letter.[8] Few writers have been more devoted in this way to language.

Galateo is informed by an intimate knowledge of the style and substance of ancient philosophy and literature. Della Casa could write in Latin with the same confidence he had in Italian (maybe more), and he translated Thucydides into Latin. Della Casa's Latin treatise *De officiis*, which has much in common with *Galateo*, is built upon classical foundations of ancient philosophy.[9] "Almost a mosaic of Greek and Latin borrowings," *Galateo* is built on Plutarch's moral treatises, the "Characters" of Theophrastus, and the educational writings of Erasmus.[10] His preferred genres were classical ones: dialogues, letters, orations, and dramas.

The style of *Galateo* echoes its own classical moral underpinnings, imitating Cicero's oratorical diction and restrained delivery as well as his moral stance. Classical decorum is punctured throughout, however, with scandalous and scabrous colloquialisms taken from the city streets of Florence. Della Casa's language mirrors the restraint and gravity of Latin prose but is filled with topical references, proverbs, and whimsical turns of phrase. The following sample may begin with a ponderous Latinate locution and allusion to two Florentine poets, but it subverts any blind allegiance to literary models many times before it ends: "Therefore, it is a nasty habit when certain people in public put their hands on whatever part of their body they wish to touch. Similarly, it is improper for a polite gentleman to arrange himself to relieve his physical needs in the sight of others. Nor, when finished, should he return to their presence still adjusting himself in his clothing" (chap. 3). The restrained and "classical" style here jars with the crude physicality of a comment on comportment that would never find its way into modern guides to etiquette.

There are moments when style seems to undercut the very manners that Della Casa is endorsing. It is certainly harsh, if not cruel, to compare, as Della Casa does, a bad speaker to a deaf-mute struggling to tell a story. *Galateo* is not only a very thoughtful book but one distinguished by immediacy, spontaneity, inhibition, and recourse to afterthoughts. Another signature feature of *Galateo* noted by Italian critics is its relentless, even ruthless, negativity; on the one hand, Della Casa wants to teach us how to act properly, how to behave appropriately, but he seems, on the other, to have only the negative example at his disposal. This negative energy is felt keenly in the original Italian, with its double-negative constructions, frequent use of "neither . . . nor," and bold imperatives. Like the nagging parent who forgets to say one thing positive, but in the extreme becomes more amusing, more sincere, and perhaps more humane, so the narrator in *Galateo* achieves remarkable power and character by dictating what *not* to do.

As we read *Galateo* today, we must remember that Della Casa was, in the view of most people of his time, the finest poet writing between Tasso and Ariosto. His prose is distinguished by a poet's sense of rhythms and emphasis and careful use of ideas and images. Relatively unknown and rarely translated into English, Della Casa's poetry has been the subject of extensive commentary in Italy.[11]

The moral basis of *Galateo* is highly social, light-years from the moral vision of Dante and Petrarch, with their solitude, prayer, saints, and soul searching. Della Casa makes no reference whatsoever to canon law or religious creeds, much less to overarching principles of Christian love and charity. He makes a few passing nods, as it were, to God. Of the scores of learned references and allusions, there is not a single reference to the Bible. Rather, he derives his vision of morality—for Della Casa manners *are* morality—from the social networks of life, the various occasions when we are called on to be *seen* and *heard*.

Even the forms of classical writing Della Casa prefers involve dialogues and conversations, both social forms of writing. Della Casa was one of the founding members of the Accademia Degli Umidi, which would later become the Accademia Fiorentina, a sort of alternative university where learned members would meet to discuss philosophy, write poetry, and make connections. It was an unguarded atmosphere conducive to the pastime or game of literature. In some of these academies, poems were produced "live," skits and plays were improvised, and there would be music and, as some sources suggest, other "illicit" behaviors. In fact, Della Casa himself wrote several obscene poems. He was very much a public poet here and later in his career as a diplomat, for which he depended on his connection to

Alessandro Farnese, a cardinal and diplomat, a great patron of the arts, and the grandson of Pope Paul III. So while Della Casa seems to be dealing with mere politeness and questions of "decorum" and of "propriety," these very acts are by no means frivolous or inconsequential. On the contrary, they might be necessary for landing a job or maintaining a social advantage.

Historians have suggested that the complex codes of behavior that we find in these Italian conduct guides could emerge only in very regulated, homogenous environments, such as the Vatican palace or the Renaissance courts. But even when Della Casa talks of "households" in *Galateo*, he is referring not merely to a private family but to a public circle that includes guests, honored or not, courtiers, friends of friends, and servants. The scenes of *Galateo* are public ones, at the dinner table, on the street, meeting people, at work, or at social events; extraordinary attention is paid to looking good, making a good first impression, not giving offense, and, especially, conversation:

> If you don't make light of my instruction, you will never find yourself caught saying, "Come right in, Mr. Agostino," to someone whose name is actually Agnolo or Bernardo; and you will not be forced to say, "Remind me, what was your name again," or say over and over again, "I'm not putting it very well," nor "Gosh, how can I say it," nor stammer nor stutter at length in order to remember some word: "Mr. Arrigo, no, Mr. Arabico. What am I saying? Mr. Agapito!" (chap. 23)

Galateo is implicitly a commentary on proper spoken, written, and poetic language, as well as a defense of the admired literary talents of two centuries earlier. As in Castiglione's *Book of the Courtier* and Stefano Guazzo's *Civil Conversation*, much attention is paid to the effective use of language, to jokes and storytelling, to vulgar language and euphemism, and to the "lost art" of conversation.[12]

At times, the subtleness of Della Casa's suggestions implicates the reader in the illicit behavior, as if the "certain people" he describes as acting inappropriately might be people we know. Notice how the author categorically denounces the use of curses and dirty words here, while being tempted to use them himself: "Nor should you talk about something dirty, even though it could be pretty amusing to hear, for decent people should try to please others only with respectable subjects. Neither in jest nor seriously should you say anything against God or his saints, no matter how witty and clever it seems" (chap. 11).

THE WORLD AS STAGE AND RENAISSANCE SELF-FASHIONING

The first English version of *Galateo*, which we can easily imagine Shakespeare reading as a twelve-year-old boy, appeared in a translation by Robert Peterson in 1576. Behind Polonius in Hamlet (1609), with his tedious "neither a borrower nor a lender be," stands the tedious uncle who narrates *Galateo*.

Della Casa's treatise would have been immediately recognized by the literate society of Shakespeare's London as akin to several other brilliant literary imports from Italy, including Ludovico Ariosto's *Orlando furioso* (1561) in Sir John Harrington's translation (1591), Torquato Tasso's *Gerusalemme conquistata* (1593), translated by Edward Fairfax (1600), and Giovanni Battista Guarini's *Il pastor fido* (1590), translated by

John Dymock (1602). Shakespeare scholar Bruce Smith has pointed out that "a visit to the bookstalls in St. Paul's churchyard in 1602 would have turned up 'self-help' books in numbers quite proportionate to what bookstores display today."[13] Could Della Casa have contributed in some measure to English Renaissance theater? Think, for example, of the great humorous characters created by Shakespeare: Benedict, Malvolio, Sir Toby Belch, Jacques, Shylock, Dogberry, Bottom, and Falstaff. All of them are most entertaining when they take things dead seriously. In every case, it is the extremely specific breach of etiquette, good taste, or discretion (the yellow stockings and garters of Malvolio, for example) that pushes them over into the world of comic excess. Della Casa even instructs us on how *not* to laugh:

> One should not laugh like a buffoon, nor in a boisterous or an insipid way, nor laugh out of habit rather than need. And I do not want you to laugh at your own jokes, for this is a type of self-praise. It is the hearer who should laugh, not the speaker. I do not want to make you believe that since each one of these things represents only a small error, they are, all together, a small error. In fact, out of many little mistakes one big one is made, as I said at the beginning. The smaller they are, the closer others will scrutinize them, for they are not easily perceived, and they sneak into our habits without our noticing them. (chap. 30)

Della Casa's catalogs of unappealing gestures and thoughtless, involuntary actions could be addressed to an actor trying to play a role. What if there were an audience observing every single move we made? This memorable passage ends with a vivid image that could be out of pastoral comedy: "It is not proper either to show one's tongue, or stroke one's beard too much as many have gotten into the habit of doing, or rub your hands together, or sigh, or moan, or twitch, or move in fits and starts, which is what some people do, or stretch out, and while stretching sound off with pleasure, 'Oh my! Oh my!' like a yokel waking up in a haystack" (chap. 30).

Della Casa advises the nobleman *never* to run in the street. We must constantly operate as if we are before an audience.

"MADE AS A JOKE"

Galateo has for too long been viewed, in the words of Claudia Berra, as "too serious with respect to how the work was for its author)."[14] In the end, Della Casa's *Galateo* is not only a work about conformity and law, perfection and rules, but also an exasperated, amazed, and sometimes theatrical reaction to the diverse ways people make fools of themselves. On one level, it is a very amusing work.

This comic tendency in Florence, inspired by and closely imitative of classical tendencies in humor, embraced the coarse and popular story and, not to a small degree, the crude and obscene joke. The most important joke collection was gathered by Poggio Bracciolini (1380–1459):

Petrarch, in his *Rerum memorandarum libri* (1343–45), wrote down the following passage from Macrobius' *Saturnalia* II. 2. 10: "The famous painter Lucius Mallius had ugly children. A friend dining with him, on seeing the children: 'Your children are not as pretty as your pictures.' Mallius replied: 'That's true.

The painting were made in the daylight, but the children in the dark.'"[15]

In a letter dated 29 January 1559, Annibale Rucellai, the nephew to whom *Galateo* was likely addressed, says that *Galateo* was written as a rhetorical exercise: "*Galateo* was made only as a joke and to see how our language would tolerate a humble and modest style, and I know that it was not esteemed by its author as a thing of great moment."[16] The style of *Galateo* is simultaneously hyperserious and highly comic. Gennaro Barbarisi, one of the important Italian scholars of Galateo, sees the treatise as caught between the silly and the very serious.[17] Della Casa is the kind of comedian who himself never laughs, sometimes can't even smile, the kind who unnerves us at times by not letting us in on the joke.

Renaissance English and Latin translations seem to have downplayed *Galateo*'s more entertaining aspects. Richard Graves, however, in his introduction to the book in 1774, called attention to the comedy in Della Casa's prose, realizing that the utility of the work coexists with its entertainment value: "It may be said, perhaps, that many of the precepts here delivered (especially the former part of the Treatise) are ridiculous; and cautions against indelicacies, which no one of any education can, in this age, be guilty of." He continues: "I defy any man to read many of his reflections with a serious countenance: not to mention the merit those little satirical strokes have (like the characters of Theophrastus) in giving a curious picture of the affectations and fopperies of the age, in which they were written."[18] Graves was so taken by the highly amusing character of *Galateo* that he introduced it with several amusing anecdotes, adding as well some footnotes to other jokes and, rightly, comic scenes in Seneca.

Although Della Casa never revealed his intentions in writing *Galateo*, there is one document that justifies viewing *Galateo* as an elaborate, ironic exercise in comic-serious style. There is an interplay of written and spoken languages, local connotations of comic words, comic timing, rhetorical excesses (the opening is too presumptuous to be anything but ironic), understatement, some elements of quite blatant mockery (uneasily sharing the pages with admonitions against scoffing and slander), invective (another Florentine form), extremely subtle use of vulgarity (with instances from Dante, no less), a remarkably nuanced lampoon of would-be comedians and punsters, with examples of those jokes that are funny mostly because the person telling them is such an ass.

Della Casa distinguishes (in chap. 20, for example) those who can tell jokes from those who only think they can. An analysis of this section would require an essay in itself, but essentially Della Casa creates dramatic characters to expose those people who may amuse themselves but are really just annoying to everyone else, characters who pun and have no sense of comic timing or true wit.

BEAUTY, CHARM, AND MEASURE IN DAILY LIVING

The right action for Della Casa is rarely distinguished from the one that satisfies the sense apparatus. The conscience cannot be detached from the aesthetic principles of pleasure, beauty, perspective, balance, moderation, good taste, symmetry, and form. It is almost as if a specific behavior is not so much wrong as it is offensive to anyone with an eye for beauty—and so much the worse for it. Toward the close of the work, Della Casa discourages playing a wind instrument, no matter how nice the tune sounds, simply on the grounds that tooting makes you look so silly.

Throughout his rambling treatise, in highly inventive and often quite amusing ways, Della Casa exposes moral depravity in the form of physical ugliness, gawky postures, and, of course, bodily functions. His writing is often so direct, earthy, and candid as to unsettle modern readers in our more "sensitive" times. The cover of a recent Italian edition of *Galateo* captures this perfectly:

> Can you achieve the beauty of a Greek sculpture just by sitting at a dinner table? Or talking about this and that with a person met by chance? The pages of Monsignor Giovanni Della Casa are here, after five hundred years, to show us that you can. They show that grace and proportion are not only in bodies and in nature but in every fold of human action. Never rebel against the custom, whatever it be. Speak in a courteous way and dress fashionably, without attracting attention. Do not use vulgar words and indecent language. And do not be verbose and pompous, much less vacant and silent. Do not claim the right, even when you're right. Because there is neither right nor wrong: there is only what matters at the moment.[19]

The narrator rarely appeals to moral absolutes or perfect embodiments of goodness in the form of classical or religious heroes; those admirable men mentioned at several points seem made of flesh and blood. They are like the Renaissance portraits of Bronzino or Pontormo or Titian, artists working in the same moment with their passive and beautifully self-controlled gazes.

Della Casa accepts the standard moral postures of classical Greece—the *mediocritus* of Aristotle—but he is no moral theorist. The gauge for how we should behave is not intellectual/theoretical but rather social/psychological. We determine appropriate action by eye and ear, good behavior by the outcomes of experience in daily life, and good conduct by an acute knowledge of social context.

A PSYCHOLOGY OF POLITENESS

Della Casa considers the implications of being trapped in a body with orifices. On the one hand he seems to reduce the gentleman to the level of a beast, but on the other the points of similarity —halitosis, dirty nostrils, and evacuation—remain entirely figments of the gentleman's hyperactive imagination.

Underlying the text there seems to be an intense fear of being embarrassed or mocked or of otherwise looking or speaking like a fool. Although some scholars have contended that *Galateo* is about the search for ideals and for the ideal courtier, the picture is more of caricatured customs and ordinary examples of what is gross, obnoxious, and bothersome. In the search for moderation above all things, the author seems obsessed with how narrow the middle road is and with exposing the excesses and perversions of individuals.

Embarrassment is instigated not by reality but by a prefabrication on the stage of the creative mind: "Nor, in my opinion, when returning [from the toilet], should he even wash his hands if in the presence of decent company, since the reason for washing himself will reveal in their imaginations some-thing repulsive." And in the same chapter, he says it is entirely inappropriate to smell someone's food or drink. "Besides, I would not want someone to sniff even what he himself has to drink or to eat," Della Casa writes; "the reason is that from his nose could fall those things that men find disgusting, even though this is perhaps unlikely" (chap. 3).

By gazing on the superficies of human behavior, Della Casa does not, as one might expect, overlook or downplay our mys-terious interior. Again, he ingeniously complicates any fac-ile distinctions between the inner and the outer person; he continually acknowledges the effect sensual data have on the psychological, even emotional, state of human beings. This awareness of sensual sympathy pervades the book in various ways, as when with poetic imagination Della Casa observes the effects of watching someone eating bitter fruit. Della Casa cre-ates a sort of psychological physics of attraction and repulsion, based entirely on the tiniest error in discretion, oversight, or loss of self-control. For example, the narrator (in chap. 2) straightforwardly asserts the sensual basis of his conception of good and evil, virtue and vice: "Let us say, then, that every act which annoys any of the senses, and that is contrary to desire, and that the imagination represents as a filthy thing, or similarly that which the mind finds repulsive, is unpleasant and one must not do it." Even that most powerful bond called love, Della Casa suggests, can be broken in an instant by an ill-advised breach of behavior, like spitting: "This is a nauseating habit not likely to make anyone love you, but rather, if someone loved you, he or she would fall out of love right there" (chap. 3).

We realize how much of our everyday behavior is regulated

by an extremely subtle code of corporeal rules, with implications and contingencies. The risks of motion are myriad, while lack of it is catatonic stupor. Should the stiff, iron-clad poses held in Italian Renaissance portraits—there is one by Pontormo long thought to be of Della Casa himself—be viewed in the light of this critique of bodily motion?

Della Casa, trying to prevent his nephew from becoming a laughingstock, recommends repeatedly that we should refrain from any extreme or odd movement. Throughout the book, rapid or uncontrolled motions are aligned with the funny, the ugly, and the unacceptable. Consider, for example, Della Casa's injunction not to touch any part of the body that is clothed. Here Della Casa evokes the character who is perpetually trying to be the life of the party, reducing him to a ridiculous and unattractive figure moving about: "These are movements of the mind, and if they are pleasant and lively they are an indication and a testimonial of the nimble mind and the good habits of the speaker—this is particularly liked by other men and endears us to them. But if they are without grace and charm, they have the contrary effect, so it appears a jackass is joking, or that someone very fat with an enormous butt is dancing and hopping about in a tight-fitting vest" (chap. 20).

CIVILITY NOW

Giovanni Della Casa would be shocked to see *Galateo* shelved, as it is in most libraries today, alongside books by Amy Vanderbilt and Emily Post. In our time, the word *etiquette* alone summons up images of finishing schools, regulations for place settings, bridesmaids' gifts, and formal invitations to showers. Della Casa has almost nothing at all in common with this notion of etiquette. Indeed, he has very little to say regarding these protocols.

His focus is rather on admiring particular actions and mocking or lampooning those singular actions that cause ignominy or should cause humiliation. Throughout *Galateo*, there is a tension between the apparently frivolous nature of the subject and the seriousness with which it is treated. Pushed forward to our time, his subject is the infuriating woman on the rapid transit train putting on her makeup, someone on the park bench flossing his teeth, people who insist on tapping their feet during a chamber recital, snobs who chat or conduct business on their cell phones in the art museum, and anyone gross who, like Sir Toby Belch, who excuses himself by saying, "Damn these pickled herring!" And to see these actions as laughable—but also somehow very unacceptable—requires self-restraint and self-analysis.

If Della Casa and Castiglione are no longer read as much as they once were, their books are, as Samuel Johnson put it, "neglected only because they have effected that reformation which their authors intended, and their precepts now are no longer wanted. Their usefulness to the age in which they were written is sufficiently attested by the translations which almost all the nations of Europe were in haste to obtain." There is some evidence in recent years that the reformation intended is wearing off. Frequent are editorials and commentaries on rude behavior, a lack of common courtesy, the absence of self-control, and the deterioration of social skills in our culture. A "charm offensive" has been launched in England; the National Institute for Civil Discourse has been established at the University of Arizona; Johns Hopkins University has also launched a civility program.[20]

Galateo is not only a book to put in the mailbox of your rude neighbors, or to hand to a sour colleague, or to recommend to the generally disgruntled among us. It is a treatise to give to your "dearest child," as Della Casa did, to show the experience he had gained over an extraordinarily busy and active political and social life. So what we have in this book of the strange title is a guide to good living, civility, and decency of conduct. It is not written from the point of view of someone overly sensitive, full of empathy and tact, but rather by a Renaissance poet with an eye toward Platonic forms of Beauty and Leon Battista Alberti's notion of measure and symmetry. It is a book about the nature of humor. It is a conduct manual, a viable tourist guide to acting Italian in Italy, and a learned analysis of literary language. It is the great source of all twentieth-century conduct guides, to be read and followed carefully, so as not to give offense at a dinner party. Della Casa challenges the notion that by becoming *less* polite and concerned for others, we become *more* free. On the contrary, *Galateo* reminds us that only by obeying such restrictions can we achieve liberty, "which is what one desires above everything" (chap. 17).

HOW GIOVANNI DELLA CASA'S
GALATEO GOT HERE

Galateo was enormously popular during the Renaissance. Within two years of its publication in Venice in 1558, editions appeared in Milan, Florence, Rome, and Bologna. Della Casa's work captured and stimulated the collective imagination of the age, quickly spreading well beyond the walls of Florence and the lagoons of Venice. It was enthusiastically received, first in France (translated by Jean du Peyrat, 1562), then in Spain (translated by Domingo Bezerra, 1585), then in Germany (1607).

In one of the six preliminary poems—three in English, one in Latin, two in Italian – prefacing the first English edition of *Galateo*, Thomas Drant captured in plodding rhyme the swift cultural transmission of this text:

> This book by Tyber, and by Po hath past,
> Through all Italia Townes and Country lands.
> Iberus, throughe thy Spanishe coasts as fast,
> It after yoade: and Gauls it held in hands,
> Throughe Rhenus realms it spred in Prosperous speede,
> To Lordes and Ladies reading comly reede.

Galateo was issued in a bilingual edition (Italian and French, Lyons, 1583), a four-language edition (Italian, French, Latin, and Spanish, 1598), and even a five-language edition (1608).

The book's appeal continued into the seventeenth century. It appeared in English or Spanish dress, in such popular versions as Nathaniel Walker's *The Refined Courtier* (1663) and the Spaniard Lucas Gracián Dantisco's *The Spanish Galateo*, first published in Tarragona in 1593. The 1707 publication in Florence of the first collected works of Della Casa by Giambattista Casotti triggered even more enthusiasm for *Galateo*. Casotti's three volumes were followed, among numerous popular printings, by a five-volume edition of Della Casa's writings in Venice, a six-volume edition in Naples, a version in Latin by Francesco Dandino, and one in Portuguese. A verse "imitation" in a strange Venetian patois (Venice, 1751) survives in only one documented copy, today at the New York Public Library. In the eighteenth century, *Galateo* was often abridged and attached to other works, for example, to the *Letters* of Lord Chesterfield.

It was toward the end of the eighteenth century that *Galateo* began to fall out of critical favor. In the United States, *Galateo* was published for the first time in Baltimore in 1811, using without acknowledgment the translation of Graves. It was printed along with John Trusler's *The Honours of the Table; or, Rules for Behavior during Meals; with the Whole Art of Carving* (1788), an amusing and useful guide to choosing and slicing different meats. "To the real artist in humanity, what are called bad manners are often the most picturesque and significant of all," Walt Whitman said, suggesting that politeness had acquired a negative connotation. *Galateo* continues to be read and studied in Italy. As Graves noted back in 1774, "it is almost proverbial description to say of an ill-bred fellow . . . that he has not read 'Il Galateo.'"

NOTE ON THE TEXT AND TRANSLATION

Samuel Butler said that a translator "dyes an author like an old stuff, into a new Colour, but can never give it the Beauty and Lustre of the first Tincture."

This is the first translation that presents the complete text of *Galateo*, informed by bibliographical research concerning the book's textual editing. Peterson's translation of 1776 was based on a French intermediary. Seventeenth-century editions were only truncated "versions of the original." The eighteenth century saw two translations, one composed by a committee of Oxford students, the other a wonderful achievement by the obscure Richard Graves. I have paid homage to Peterson and Graves by using a few of their phrases.

The only surviving manuscript of the work, written in the hand of a secretary and for decades not available to scholars, is contained in a codex called MS Ricci-Parracciani *RP* (Vat. Lat. 14825) in the Biblioteca Apostolica Vaticana. When after Della Casa's death the work was published in Venice by Bevilacqua in 1558, it was edited and changed from the manuscript by Erasmo Gemini and Carlo Gualteruzzi.

In 1991, Gennaro Barbarisi published a scholarly edition based on the manuscript, which led to a lively debate in Italy, one that remains unresolved. Barbarisi argued that the manuscript is written in a language more spontaneous and original, more in keeping with spoken language than the earliest published versions. Most of the changes were quite specific and would be significant only if producing a critical edition. However, this textual debate stimulated renewed interest in the style of the text, brushing off the dust of the printed editions gathered over the last century. In this translation, aimed at the common reader (scholars should consult the extensive secondary literature on *Galateo*), I have tried to give Della Casa's fabric its original natural quality and sheen.

Although not present in the manuscript sources or the first printed editions, chapter headings have been included by editors going back to excellent eighteenth-century editions of Della Casa's *Works*, published in Florence, Venice, and Naples. For the benefit of modern readers, I have done the same, although I have made them more concise than was the fashion in Enlightenment-era editions. I am indebted for the notes to the many previous editors of *Galateo*.

GALATEO

or,

THE RULES OF
Polite Behavior

1

Long-winded opening—good manners, compared with more weighty virtues, and why they are no less useful to a gentleman

Since it is the case[2] that you are now just beginning that journey that I have for the most part as you see completed, that is, the one through mortal life, and loving you so very much as I do, I have proposed to myself—as one who has been many places—to show you those places in life where, walking through them, I fear you could easily either fall or take the wrong direction.[3] And so, under my tutelage, you may stay on the right path toward the salvation of your soul as well as for the dignity and honor of your distinguished and noble family.[4] And since at such a tender age you would be incapable of grasping more abstruse or subtle lessons, reserving them for the proper season I am going to begin with what to many would seem frivolous: that is, how I believe one should behave when speaking or dealing with others, so as to be appropriate, pleasant, and polite. This is either virtue or something very like virtue.[5] And even though being liberal-minded or loyal or generous is in itself undoubtedly more important and laudable than being charming and courteous, nonetheless perhaps pleasant habits and decorous manners and words are no less useful to those who have them than a largeness of spirit and complete confidence. This is so since everyone must each day many times deal with others and converse with them daily. Justice, fortitude, and the other greater and nobler virtues are called into service more infrequently. The munificent and magnanimous are not obligated to act generously all the time, for no one could behave in this way very often. Similarly those among us who are strong and brave are required to display their valor and their noble qualities in action, but very rarely. Thus, while such talents easily surpass the former in greatness and sheer moral weight, the virtues I consider surpass the others in number and frequency. Now, if it were appropriate, I could mention to you many people who, though otherwise of little merit, nevertheless were and still are highly admired just for their pleasant and gracious manners; by these manners they have been sustained to the point of attaining high prestige, leaving very far behind those gifted with the clearer and more noble virtues I have mentioned. And just as pleasant and proper etiquette has the force to arouse benevolence in those with whom we live, so on the contrary boorish and uncouth behavior provokes others to hate and despise us. For this reason, even though no legal punishment can be meted out for the display of unpleasant and gruff manners (for these sins seem very light—and in fact are not mortal), we see nevertheless that nature rebukes us severely for them, depriving us of others' companionship and benevolence. And surely as great sins harm us, so these minor faults are annoying, and they gall us more often. And just as we fear savage beasts but have no fear of tiny insects, such as mosquitoes or flies, still, on account of the constant annoyance of these pests, we complain more often about them. Likewise, most of us hate unpleasant and bothersome people as much as evil ones, maybe even more. Because of this no one would deny that for whoever is disposed to live, not alone or in a hovel,[6] but in cities among other human beings, it is extremely useful to be in habit and manners both gracious and pleasant. Moreover, the other virtues require more furnishings or else are nothing, or useless, while these virtues on their own are rich and vigorous since they consist of words and actions only.

2

Annoying behavior defined simply in terms of sensual suffering

So that you may more easily learn to do this, you must know it is advantageous to temper and order your habits,[7] not according to your whim, but according to the pleasure of those who are around you and to whom you direct your behavior. But this you must do with moderation, for if you conform too much to the pleasure of others in your conversation or in behavior, you appear pretty much a buffoon or a jokester, or maybe even a flatterer, rather than a polite gentleman.[8] And, on the contrary, those who do not care about others' pleasure or displeasure are rude, inappropriate, and unrefined. Therefore, our manners are attractive when we regard others' pleasures and not our own delight. And if we try to investigate things that generally please the majority and those things that people find annoying, we can readily discover which actions must be avoided in social life and which we should adopt.

Let us say, then, that any act which annoys any of the senses, and that is contrary to desire,[9] and that the imagination represents as a filthy thing, or similarly that which the mind finds repulsive, is unpleasant and one must not do it.

3

Disgusting things offend the senses—and even the imagination and desire

And thus it is that in the presence of others one should not do things revolting, fetid, gross, or obnoxious, and should even avoid mentioning them. And not only is it unpleasant to do or mention such things, but you should even go so far as to avoid bringing to mind any act that really bothers people. Therefore, it is a nasty habit when certain people in public put their hands on whatever part of their body they wish to touch. Similarly, it is improper for a polite gentleman to arrange himself to relieve his physical needs in the sight of others. Nor, when finished, should he return to their presence still adjusting himself in his clothing. Nor, in my opinion, when returning, should he even wash his hands if in the presence of decent company, since the reason for washing himself will reveal in their imaginations something repulsive. And for the same reason it is not an appropriate behavior, when on the road as sometimes happens one sees something disgusting, to turn to one's companions and point it out. Even much less should one entreat someone to sniff something that stinks, as some are inclined to do with enormous insistence, even twisting up their noses and saying:

"Wow, smell this, ugh, it reeks"—; rather you should say, "Don't even breathe, it stinks." And just as these and similar actions annoy the senses they pertain to, so grinding one's teeth, or whistling, screeching, the rubbing of stones and grating of metal are unpleasant to the ear, and so one ought to abstain from such as much as you can. And not only this, but you must watch your singing, especially solo, if you are tone-deaf and sing off key. Few can resist doing this; in fact, it seems the less one's natural musical talent, the more one sings. There are some who, coughing or sneezing, make such a loud noise that others go deaf; in similar acts they are so indiscreet that those nearby get spritzed in the face. You will also find those who, yawning, bellow and bray like a donkey; or a person with his big mouth wide open who wants you to follow his point, sending out of his mouth that voice—or rather that racket—a deaf-mute makes when he attempts to tell a story. And these rude and vulgar manners you want to avoid, as they disturb the ear and the eye. Rather, a polite person ought to abstain from many yawns, and not just for the reasons cited above, but because yawning seems to come from weariness and disgust, and he who yawns would love to be anywhere else but where he is, and dislikes the group he's with, and the conversation, and the activities. And sure, even though a man is most of the time ready to yawn, should he be distracted by some delight or some thought, it doesn't come to mind to yawn, but when he is lazy and indolent he is easily induced to yawn. And so when somebody yawns in the presence of apathetic and thoughtless persons, everybody else will immediately start yawning incontinently, as you may have seen many times, as if that person had reminded them of something they would have done themselves already, had they only thought of it first. And many times have I heard learned men say that the Latin word for yawning means lethargic and careless.[10] It's advisable to flee this habit which—as I have said—is unpleasant to the eye, the ear, and the stomach; by indulging in it, we show the company around us that we are not having a good time, and we also cast a very bad impression of ourselves, that is to say, we display a drowsy, slumbering spirit. This makes us not lovable at all to those we are around. You do not want, when you blow your nose, to then open the hanky and gaze at your snot as if pearls or rubies might have descended from your brains.[11] This is a nauseating habit not likely to make anyone love you, but rather, if someone loved you, he or she would fall out of love right there. The spirit of the Labyrinth, whoever he may have been, proves this: in order to cool the ardor of Giovanni Boccaccio for a lady he barely knew, he tells how she squats down by a fireside, coughs, and spits out huge loogies.[12]

Also inappropriate is the habit of putting one's nose over the glass of wine someone else is drinking, or on top of the food others must eat, so as to smell it. Besides, I would not want someone to sniff even what he himself has to drink or to eat; the reason is that from his nose could fall those things that men find disgusting, even though this is perhaps unlikely. Nor would I recommend that you offer your glass of wine to someone after you have had your lips to it and sipped, unless it were to someone more intimate than a friend. And even worse should you offer a pear or other fruit from which you have just taken a bite. And don't be looking like you consider the things discussed above trivial and of small moment, for even light blows, if they are many, can kill.

4

Galateo and Count Ricciardo—an anecdote on the importance of politeness

I want you to know that in Verona there was once a bishop, very learned in the great books and profoundly wise, named Giovanni Matteo Giberti.[13] Aside from his other admirable qualities, he was also courteous and generous with the nobles who came and went about him, honoring them at home with his magnificence, not in excess but as a golden mean befitting a cleric. It so happened that a nobleman by the name of Count Ricciardo was just then passing through and stayed several days with the bishop and his household, which was composed, for the most part, of urbane and educated men.[14] Because the count seemed to them a very refined gentleman, adorned with pleasant manners, they praised and esteemed him highly, except for one trifling imperfection in his behavior. The bishop, a discerning man, noticed it and, having sought the advice of some of his closer friends, decided that the count ought to be made aware of it, without causing him any undue stress. Since the count was set to depart the following morning and had already taken his leave, the bishop summoned a discreet gentleman of his household and told him to ride out and accompany the count part of the way and then, when he thought the time was right, to tell him very sweetly what they had discussed. This gentleman was a man up in years, very learned, as well as pleasant, a good conversationalist and handsome, all beyond belief, who in his time had much frequented the noble courts. He was and perhaps still is called Mr. Galateo, and it was at his bidding and on his advice that I first started to compose this treatise.[15] Riding with the count, he soon engaged him in pleasant chat, passing from one topic to the next, until it seemed time to return to Verona. Asking for permission to take his leave of the count with a cheerful look, he said delicately: "My lord, my lord bishop extends your lordship his infinite thanks for the honor you have bestowed upon him by entering and dwelling in his humble abode. Furthermore, as recompense for all the courtesy you have shown toward him he has commanded me to present you with a gift on his behalf. And he earnestly entreats you to receive it with a glad heart. This is the gift. The bishop thinks you are the most graceful and well-mannered gentleman he has ever met. For this reason, having carefully observed your manners and having examined them with more than ordinary attention, he has found none which was not extremely pleasant and laudable, except for one that is deformed: the unseemly action your lips and mouth make when chewing food at table makes a strange smacking kind of sound very unpleasant to hear. The bishop sends you this message, begging you to try to abstain from doing this and to accept as a precious gift his loving reprimand and remark, for he is certain no one else in the world would give you such a present." The count, who had never before been aware of his faux pas, blushed a bit on being chastised, but being a worthy man he quickly pulled himself together and said: "Please tell the bishop that men would be far richer than they are if all gifts exchanged were like his. And thank him kindly for all the courtesy and benevolence he has afforded me, assuring him that from now on I will diligently and attentively watch myself. Now go, and Godspeed."

5

Returning to the subject of offensive and gauche habits

Well, what do we think the bishop and his noble comrades would have said to those we sometimes see who, absolutely oblivious as pigs with their snouts in the swill, never raise their faces nor their eyes, much less their hands, from the food? And they gulp down their grub with both their cheeks puffed out as if they were playing the trumpet or blowing on a fire, not eating but gobbling. Those who grease up their hands and arms to the elbows or dirty their napkins such that washcloths in the bathroom are neater. Often they shamelessly use these same napkins to wipe away sweat that, from their rushing and gorging, drips and falls from their foreheads, their faces, and from around their necks, even using them to blow their noses when they feel like it. Truly people made like this are not worthy of being invited, not only to the immaculate house of that noble bishop, but they should even be chased out of any place where civilized men dwell. A man of good manners must therefore watch himself that he does not smear his fingers so much with grease that his napkin is left filthy: it is a disgusting sight. And even wiping fingers on the bread you are eating does not seem very proper or polite. The noble servants who wait on gentlemen's tables must not, under any circumstance, scratch their heads or anywhere else in front of their master when he is eating, nor put their hands on any part of the body that one covers up, nor even appear to do so, as some sloppy servants do, who keep a hand on the chest or behind the back tucked under their clothing. They must rather display their hands in the open and outside of any suspicion, and keep them carefully washed and clean, with nothing grimy on any part. Those who serve the plates and the glasses must diligently abstain during that moment from spitting, from coughing, and moreover from sneezing. Because, in such actions, suspicion of misbehavior is as annoying to diners as certainty, so the servants must take care not to give their masters reason to be suspicious, for in this case what might have taken place disturbs as much as what has. If you have placed a pear to cook by the fireplace or a piece of toast on the coals, do not blow on it because it is covered with a bit of ash, for as the saying goes: *There never was wind without rain.*[16] You must rather tap the plate, or by some other means brush off any ashes. Do not offer your handkerchief, even fresh from the laundry, to anyone, as the person will not know it's clean and so will find the act gross. When speaking with someone, do not get so close as to puff on the person's face, for you will find that many do not like to inhale someone else's breath, even though there may be no bad odor. These and other such behaviors are unpleasant and should be avoided for they irritate the senses of those we interact with, as I said above.

Let us now mention some breaches of etiquette that, without being offensive to any one sense in particular, offend the vast majority of people when they are committed.

6

Ways we enjoy one another, and irk one another, especially in conversation

You must realize that humans by nature have appetites for many and various things. Some want to vent their wrath, some satisfy their gluttony, others indulge their libido, others their pure greed, still others a different urge. But in dealing with them, it does not seem that one asks for, or is able to ask for, or desires any of the above-mentioned vices. These appetites do not consist in the manners or fashions or speech of people, but in something else entirely. People actually desire whatever can facilitate communicating with each other; and this seems to be goodness, honor, and serenity, or something else quite similar. For this reason one must never say or do anything that gives the impression that one has little affection for or appreciation of others. This is exhibited by the very impolite tendency of many people to fall asleep in the middle of a pleasant group sitting together in conversation. By doing this, they demonstrate, in effect, how little they think of the others and how little they appreciate them and their conversation. Not to mention that whoever falls asleep, particularly in an uncomfortable position, which invariably occurs, tends most of the time to commit some act unpleasant to see or to hear. Very often such sleepy folks wake up sweaty and drooling. For this same reason getting yourself up while others are sitting and talking and then pacing around the room seems a bothersome habit. There are yet others who are continually fidgeting, twitching, stretching out, and yawning, turning first to one side and then to the other, so it looks as if they have in that instant caught a fever: such is clear evidence that they regret being in that company. Those who occasionally pull a letter out of their pocket to read are equally rude. Worse yet is the one who brings out a fingernail scissor and devotes herself to clipping or filing her nails, treating the others like they are worth nothing, amused to find some other distraction in order to pass the time. One must not adopt the habits of some people, such as humming a tune, or imitating the beating of a drum on the table with their fingers, or shuffling their legs, for these actions indicate a real contempt for others. In addition, one must not turn one's back on someone, nor lift one's leg high so that we see a part that clothes should conceal, for these obnoxious acts should not be committed among persons one reveres. True enough, if a gentleman acted so among very close friends or in the presence of a friend of lower social rank, he would show not arrogance but rather love and intimacy. A man must stand with an erect posture and not lean against or overtop someone else. When you speak, don't be poking others with your elbow, as many are in the habit of doing with every word, saying, "Is that not so?," "What do you think of that?," "And Mr. Whatshisname?," and all the while continuing to jab with the elbow.

7

Dressing for success

Dress nicely and according to your status and your age; by doing any less you appear to value other people too little. For this reason the citizens of Padua used to get all bent out of shape when some Venetian gentleman would stroll about their city in a simple long robe, almost as if he wanted to appear to be in his home county. Not only should one's suit be of fine material, but a man must also try to adapt himself as much as he can to the wardrobe of other citizens and let custom guide him, even though it may seem to him less comfortable and attractive than previous fashions. And if everyone in your town wears his hair in a bowl cut, you should not wear an ostentatiously long layered look; nor where the locals all sport a beard should you cut yours off.[17] This is a way of contradicting others, and such contradictions in your dealings with others should be avoided except in cases of necessity, as we will talk about later. This, more than any other bad habit, renders us despicable to the majority of people. You should not, therefore, oppose common custom in practices of this kind but rather adapt yourself to them with moderation, so that you will not be the only one in the neighborhood to wear a long gown down to your heels while everyone else dresses in an extremely short one, just below the belt. It is like having a face so incredibly dog-ugly, that is to say, something so against the order of nature that everybody turns around to stare at it. So it is also with those who do not dress according to the prevailing style but according to their own taste, with gorgeous long hair, or with a very short-cropped beard or clean shaven, or who wear tight knit caps or great big berets according to the German style. Everyone turns around to gawk at them and circles around to see them, as one does, for example, with those types who seem ready to knock out every man in the town where they live. Clothes must also fit well and suit the individual, for those who wear expensive and noble clothes either poorly made or just not suitable to who they are are indicating one of two things: either they have no notion that they could please or displease others, or they have no conception whatsoever of grace or measure. And so with their manners these men make their companions feel held in low esteem, and so they are neither warmly welcomed by most groups nor prized at all.

8

Petulant and pompous and self-serving people

Then there are certain people, beyond those mentioned, who emit an air of rudeness: for they act and behave in such a manner that it is impossible to bear them. They always cause delay, annoyance, and discomfort to the entire group; they are never ready, never organized, and never satisfied. When everybody is prepared to sit down to dinner, for example, and the meal is about to be served, and everybody has washed their hands, this one asks for a pen and paper, or he has to urinate, or she regrets having missed mass today. Or he says: "It's still so early"; "Surely you can wait a little while"; "What's the rush this morning?" And they hold everyone hostage by being concerned too much with themselves and their own needs, totally oblivious to others. Moreover they want to have it better than everyone else in every way; they want to sleep in the most comfortable bed, in the nicest room, to sit in the most comfortable chair at the head of the table, and they must be served or seated first. They don't care for anything unless they themselves thought it up, turning up their noses at everything else, and they think that others ought to wait for them before eating, going out for a ride, playing a game, or having fun. Some other people are so choleric and crabby and strange that nothing can be done to please them, and they always answer with a grimace; no matter what is said to them, they never stop reprimanding or scolding or heckling their servants, and they keep the whole company in a constant state of tribulation. "What's with waking me up so early this morning?"; "Look how you shined my shoes"; and more; "And you didn't come to church with me"; "You scumbag, I don't know what's keeping me from cracking you right between the eyes!" These kinds of expostulations are rude and must be avoided like death itself, for even if a man were humble and acted like this, not maliciously but out of carelessness and bad habit, he would be loathed all the same: his behavior would imply he was an arrogant jackass, and for that alone he would be detested. Arrogance is nothing but lack of respect for others, and, as I said at the beginning, everybody wishes to be respected even if he does not deserve it. Not long ago there was in Rome a very worthy man gifted with an astute mind and profound learning whose name was Ubaldino Bandinelli.[18] This man used to say that whenever he came to or went from the Vatican palace, although the streets were full of courtiers, prelates, and lords, and likewise of poor, or middle-class, or even low-class people, nonetheless he never thought he met anyone who was any more or less worthy than he was. Undoubtedly there were few he could have seen who would match him, keeping in mind his own virtue, which was great beyond measure. However, in such matters men must not be judged in this way; rather, they must be weighed with a farmer's scale, not the scale of a goldsmith. And it's best to be disposed to accept them readily not for what they are truly worth, but rather, as with money, for their stated value.[19] Nothing therefore must be done in front of those people we wish to please which denotes lordship rather than companionship. Every action of ours, instead, must suggest reverence and respect toward the company we keep. For this reason, any action not blameworthy done at the proper time may be reprehensible in some other context, or with other individuals, such as speaking roughly to servants, or reprimanding them as we mentioned above, or, worse still, smacking them. For doing such things is a way of ruling over someone and exercising one's power, something no one does in front of those one respects without creating a scandal and putting a quick end to the conversation, especially if it is done at the dinner table, a place for happy times and not for making a scene. Thus Currado Gianfigliazzi acted politely when he did not persist in chatter with his cook, Chichibio, so as not to disturb the guests, even though the servant deserved a severe punishment, having chosen, rather than to please his lord, to satisfy Brunetta. If Currado had made even less fuss, he would have been even more commendable, for it was not right to make threats, using the Lord's name in vain as he did.[20] But returning to our subject, I say that it is not pleasant to lose one's temper at table, no matter what happens. If one should become upset, one should not show it or give any indication of being perturbed, for the reason I have already mentioned, especially if strangers are at the table, since one invited them to enjoy themselves and now they are gloomy. It is just like when we see other people eat tart fruit and our own mouths pucker up, so the sight of others getting on edge and upset troubles us too.

9

How to spoil a conversation

Those people who want always the opposite thing are called disagreeable, as the word itself implies: for "disagreeable" is as much as to say "contrary." So the effect this has on winning the hearts of others you can easily judge for yourself, since it consists in opposing others' pleasures and tending to make enemies of them, rather than friends. Those who would force themselves to escape this vice must be worried about other people, for ornery behavior produces neither pleasure nor benevolence, but rather hatred and annoyance. In fact, make other people's desires your own, where there is no danger or shame. Act and speak with an eye toward others, rather than to yourself. One should not be either uncouth or odd, but pleasant and kind: there is no difference between the myrtle and the butcher's-broom except that one is a houseplant, the other a spiny weed. And you know a man is considered pleasant if his manners conform to the common practices among friends, whereas someone who is eccentric will, in all situations, appear to be a stranger, that is, a foreigner. On the contrary, men who are affable and polite will appear to have friends and acquaintances wherever they go. For this reason it usually behooves you to greet, chat, and answer gracefully, and to treat everyone like your neighbor or friend. Those who are never nice to anyone behave wrongly when they gladly say no thanks to everything and don't appreciate any compliment or kind turn rendered to them. They are like foreigners and barbarians. They don't put up with visitors, nor do they care for company; they are not amused by jokes or pleasantries and shrug off any offers of friendship. To "So-and-so asked me to tell you he said hello," they answer: "What does he want from me now?" Or if someone says, "So-and-so was asking how you are feeling," they respond: "If he's so interested, tell him to come and feel my pulse." People of this morose stamp really don't deserve to be held dear. It is not appropriate to be always depressed or distracted in the company of others. This may be acceptable to those who have long pursued studies that are called, so I have been told, liberal or intellectual. It should not under any circumstance be permitted among ordinary people. Even those who are allowed to be constantly brooding could do us all a favor by being pensive in private.

10

On those prim and ladylike men

It is also not appropriate, especially not for men, to be susceptible and fastidious, for using manners like this with others seems less like companionship than servitude. Sure, there are those who are so dainty and hypersensitive that to live and interact with them is nothing more than finding oneself surrounded by delicate crystal, for they fear the slightest upset, and you must treat and regard them with this in mind. They become as hurt as another if mortally wounded, when you're not timely or solicitous in saying hello, visiting them, or paying your respects or responding to them. If you do not give them all their titles precisely to a letter, they protest bitterly, and deathly enmity ensues in an instant: "You called me sir— not lord"; and "Why don't you refer to me as your lordship? After all, I treat you with respect"; or "I did not have a decent seat at the table"; and "Yesterday you didn't bother to call on me, even though I visited you the day before yesterday"; "I certainly shouldn't think this is the way to treat people like me." These types truly drive people to the point of not being able to bear the sight of them, for they love themselves beyond any bound or measure, and being so enamored with themselves, they have little space left for loving others. Besides, as I said at the outset, we expect from the company of others those pleasures which we ourselves seek. To be with such mincing, prissy weaklings, whose friendship rips as easily as the finest thread, is not friendship but a type of slavery, and such company is not fun but altogether very unpleasant. Such silly and tender manners are best left to the women.[21]

11

The don'ts of conversation

In conversation one can sin in many and various ways, starting with choice of subject: it should be neither frivolous nor vile. Listeners will not pay attention or take pleasure in it, but they will scorn the talk and the talker both. Also, one must not pick a theme too subtle or too arcane, for it is exhausting to hear. Instead, one must really diligently select a topic so that no one will turn red or feel ashamed. Nor should you talk about something dirty, even though it could be pretty amusing to hear, for decent people should try to please others only with respectable subjects. Neither in jest nor seriously should you say anything against God or his saints, no matter how witty and clever it seems. This sin was often committed by the gang of noble youths in the *Decameron* with their tales, and for this they should be chastised severely by all discerning people. Remember that to gab and joke about God is not only the sign of a delinquent and impious man but also the vice of an impolite person, and it is unpleasant to hear: you will find many who flee from a place where God's name is used profanely. Not only should one speak reverently of God, but in every discussion one should avoid with disgust words that bear witness against one's life and deeds, for men hate seeing in others the vices that are their own. Similarly, it is not proper to speak of things which are critical of the present occasion with people listening, even if these criticisms, in another time and place, would be just, good, and respected. Let Friar Nastagio's sermons then not be mentioned to young women intent on fooling around, as that fine fellow who lived near San Brancazio, not far from you, used to do all the time.[22] Neither at a party nor at the table should one tell depressing tales of woe, nor mention nor call to mind wounds, maladies, deaths, and contagious illnesses, or any other suffering. And if someone else were to lapse into this sort of lugubrious conversation, one must gently and reasonably change the subject, providing one that is lighter and in good taste. Even so, I have heard an astute neighbor of mine say that men have a great need to cry as well as to laugh. He claimed that for this reason those sad stories we call tragedies were first devised, so that when performed in theaters as they were back in that age they would bring tears to the eyes of viewers, actually curing them of certain infirmities.[23] But, whatever the case, to us it is not good to cast a gloom upon those with whom we speak, especially in the place where people are gathered for a party and a good time, rather than for anguish and weeping. If there should be someone who is so infirm that he needs a good cry, the cure is simple enough: either medicate him with some hot mustard or stick him in a smoke-filled room. For this reason there is absolutely no excuse for Filostrato, who proposed telling stories full of sorrows and pangs of death when the company was interested in nothing but being entertained.[24] It is better, then, to avoid talking about morbid and melancholy things and, if necessary, to just keep quiet. Not unlike this, nothing comes from the mouths of some others except stories about their children, their wives, or their nannies, and these types are equally to blame. "Last night my kid really made me laugh!" "You will never see a cuter baby than my little Momo"; "My wife is such a . . ."; "My Cecchina says that . . . you wouldn't believe she's smart as a whip already!"[25] No one has so little to do that he has the time to respond or even pay attention to such rubbish, and so it exasperates everyone.

12

Keep your dreams to yourself

Those who painstakingly recount their dreams with great enthusiasm, making such fuss and marveling so very much that one is left completely worn out just hearing them, are doing something bad. This is especially so since, in most cases, to listen to the story of their greatest accomplishment, even if done while wide awake, would be a total waste of time. Thus, one should not annoy others with such stuff as dreams, especially since most dreams are by and large idiotic. Although I have heard it often said that the ancient sages included a great many dreams in their books, written with high wisdom and great eloquence, it is not suitable for us uneducated men and common folk to pretend to do the same in ordinary conversation. Indeed, of all the many dreams I have heard referred to, though I suffer to lend an ear to only a few, I have never heard one worth the effort of the person who broke the silence. That is, except for one a Roman named Mr. Flaminio Tomarozzo had, and this gentleman was no nitwit or blockhead but intelligent and astute.[26] And so it goes while asleep he seemed to be sitting in the house of his neighbor, a very rich apothecary, and then, for one reason or another, the mob went on a rampage and began looting the shop. One took an elixir, another a lozenge, one, one thing, another, another, and swallowed it right there and then, so that in less than an hour there was not a vial, a pill box, a carton, or a tube that was not empty and tossed off. A small beaker remained, all full of a pure and limpid liquid, which many sniffed but none would dare taste. In a short time he saw an old man of impressive stature, an old-timer with a venerable aspect, who came in and looked at the poor apothecary's empty boxes and jars, spilled and scattered about, and almost all of them broken. Catching sight of the small flask I mentioned, he picked it up and, putting it to his mouth, drank all the liquid till not a drop remained. Having done this, he left as everyone else had already. Mr. Flaminio was much taken aback by this, so, turning to the apothecary, he asked: "Sir, who was that man, and why did he drink so deeply the water in the flask that everybody else had refused?" And the apothecary responded, saying: "My son, that was the Lord God. The water which he alone drank and which everybody else, as you saw, avoided and refused was *Discretion* which, as you may have understood, no man is willing to taste for the whole world."

Dreams like this one even I could tell and listen to with pleasure and profit, for it is more like a thought brought about by alert understanding or, shall I say, a perception by the senses than the visions of a slumbering mind. But those other dreams that lack shape and make no sense—and they are the majority—we should forget and dismiss, just not those of the good and the intelligent who, even sound asleep, are wiser than the ignorant and wicked.[27]

13

Liars and braggarts and the falsely modest

Although it seems that there is nothing vainer than dreams, there is one thing which is even more futile: and it is lies. What a man has seen in dreams was some shadow or a certain feeling, but lies have no basis in either reality or the imagination. For this reason, one asks that men's ears and minds be riled by lies even less than by the reciting of dreams, even though lies are sometimes accepted as true. In the long run, liars not only are not believed, they are not listened to, like those people whose words lack substance and whose speech is pretty much blowing hot air. Know that you will meet many men who fib without intent of malice or personal advantage or without any wish to do damage or bring shame upon anybody, but because they like lying, much like someone who drinks not for thirst but because he is crapulent for the taste of wine. Others forge lies in their own favor, boasting and bragging about great accomplishments or knowledge, aggrandizing themselves and claiming to be brilliant and capable of marvelous deeds. It's also possible to lie without speaking, that is, with actions and behavior. You will see some of middle or lower class do this when they bear themselves with great solemnity and behave pompously, speaking rhetorically, or rather pontificating, eager to sit *pro tribunale* on anything and strutting about like a peacock, which is worse than death to witness. You will find some who, although they don't have much money, have so many gold chains around their necks and so many rings on their fingers and so many pins on their hats and here and there on their outfit that not Sir Chatillon-sur-Marne in France himself could like better.[28] Their manners are full of affectation and self-importance arising first from snobbery preceded by pure vanity, and you must flee these types like unpleasant and intolerable things. Remember that in many of the best cities it is forbidden by law that a wealthy man parade about attired much more gorgeously than a poor man, for it would seem that the poor are wronged when others, even in matters of appearance, show themselves to be superior to them.[29] So one must diligently take care not to fall into follies of this kind. Nor should a man boast of his nobility, his titles, his riches, least of all his intelligence. Nor should he praise at length his past deeds and accomplishments, nor those of his family. In so doing it seems that he wants either to challenge those present who show themselves to be, or who aspire to be, his equal in nobility, wealth, skill, or bravery. Nor should he oppress them if they are of lesser social rank, even seeming to chastise them for their humble origins and poverty. In both cases such behavior displeases everybody. Thus, one should neither belittle himself nor unduly exalt himself. Instead, one should subtract a little from one's merits, rather than add something to them with words, for even what is good, if flaunted, is displeasing. You should know that those who humble themselves beyond measure in their speech and refuse all honors they are clearly due show far greater arrogance than those who usurp these honors without real merit. For this reason one could go so far as to say that Giotto did not deserve the praises some showered upon him for not wanting to be called "Master," being that he was not merely a master, but without any doubt the greatest master of his day.[30] Leaving aside whether Giotto deserves praise or blame, it is clear that a man who despises what other men covet shows that he reproaches or disparages. Likewise to lightly value glory and honor, which men esteem so highly, is to glorify yourself and exalt yourself above all others. No one of sound mind would refuse precious things, unless he feels himself the possessor of other more valuable things in abundance.

For this reason we should neither boast of our advantages nor make a joke of them, for the one is to reprove others for their shortcomings, and the other is to undervalue their virtues. As far as possible, one should keep silent about oneself, and if circumstances demand us to say something, then it is a pleasing habit to speak in an unassuming manner, as I have already said. And so those who delight in pleasing others must abstain with all their power from that common habit of expressing an opinion on any subject so timorously that it is a slow death to listen to it, especially if they are considered to be intelligent. "Sir, I beg your pardon if I cannot speak on the case at hand as suitably as it might be wished. I will speak in rough terms, like the simple man I am, according to the very little that I know and my quite obvious poor abilities. I am certain your lordship will mock me afterward, but still, in order to obey your most royal wish . . ." They work the question so much, and go to such lengths without ever resolving it, that every abstruse question could have been resolved with far fewer words in a much shorter space of time than these types spend only coming to the point. Equally tedious and deceitful are those men who, in the manner of their speech and their behavior, show themselves vulgar and vile. Although it is obvious that they are entitled to precedence and to first and highest place, they will place themselves at the back. It is then an exhausting task to push them to move forward for, like an old mare jerking away from something, they are drawn continually backward. When approaching a doorway, one always has a difficult time with people such as these, for they will by no means be prevailed upon to go first. They will step aside, or across you, or retrace their steps, and then shield and protect themselves with hands and arms, so that every few steps one must engage in battle with them, interrupting otherwise pleasant conversation or the business at hand.

14.

Ceremonies, especially empty compliments, discussed

As you can see, we have named ceremonies with a foreign term,[31] as we do with things for which our own language lacks a word; for clearly our ancestors were unaware of these ceremonies and so could not give them a name. In my judgment, ceremonies are, because of their futility, very little removed from lies and dreams. Consequently, we can very easily treat them together and connect them in our treatise, seeing that the occasion to mention them has arisen. According to what a worthy man has explained to me more than once, those solemnities which the clergy use toward God and sacred things during divine services at the altar are rightly called ceremonies. But when men first began to pay respect to each other in artificial, inappropriate ways, and to address each other with titles of Sir and Lord, bowing and bending and contorting themselves as a sign of respect, and uncovering their heads, and giving themselves far-fetched titles, and kissing each other's hands as if they were sacred like a priest's, someone who did not have a name for this new, inane habit called it a ceremony. I think it was done in mockery, just as to drink and enjoy oneself is called, in a joking tone, "to triumph." This habit is certainly not native to us but foreign and barbarous, only recently brought into Italy, from where I have no clue. Our poor country, brought low and humiliated in fact and effect, expands and is honored in vain words and superficial titles. If we consider the intention of those who use them, ceremonies are an empty show of honor and reverence toward the person to whom they are addressed, consisting of appearances, words, titles, and empty salutations. I say vain insofar as we honor in our sight those whom we have no reverence for and even, at certain times, we hold in contempt. Nevertheless, in order not to stray from the habit of others, we refer to them as "the most illustrious Sir So-and-so" and "the most excellent Lord Such-and-such." Similarly, we sometimes present ourselves as "most humble servants" to those we would prefer to do a disservice to rather than serve. Ceremonies should then be seen not simply as lies, as I have said, but also as infamies and treacheries. But since the addresses and titles I have mentioned have lost their strength and, like iron, had their temper broken by our constant use, one should not listen to them with the attention given to other words, nor rigorously interpret them. This is manifestly true in the lives of everyone, as when we meet someone we have never seen before and it happens we must speak to him without knowing his actual rank. More often than not, we would rather say too much than too little. Thus, we will call him "sir" or "gentleman," even if he is merely a shoemaker or a barber dressed decently enough. In the past, titles were determined and distinguished by privilege of the pope or emperor. These titles could not be withheld without outrage and injury to the bearer, nor, on the contrary, could they be attributed without mockery to those who did not merit them. Similarly, nowadays, one must grant these titles and other similar indications of honor much more liberally because custom, far too powerful a man, has generously endowed the men of our times with them. This habit, then, so beautiful and becoming on the outside, is totally vacuous inside, and consists in appearances without substance and words without substance. We are not allowed, however, to alter it, but rather we are obliged to abide it, as this is a fault of the times, not of ourselves. Ceremonies, however, must be carried out with discretion.

15

Three kinds of compliments—why not to extend them

For this reason one should keep in mind that compliments are paid for gain, for vanity, or out of duty. Every lie told for one's own profit is a fraud, a sin, and a dishonest thing, for one never lies honestly; this is the sin committed by flatterers who, under pretense of friendship, counterfeit and turn pimps to our lusts, whatever they may be, not because we want them to but for their own ends, not to please us but to deceive us. And although this vice may appear to be a pleasant custom, since it is in itself abominable and noxious, decent men have nothing to do with it; for it is not acceptable that one should give pleasure by offending. Because ceremonies are, as we have said, lies and false flatteries, whenever we use them for our own gain we behave as disloyal rascals: for this reason, no ceremony should be used.

16

Compliments done for vanity and out of duty, and a warning about adulation

There remains for me to speak of those ceremonies done for duty and those done out of vanity. In no way is it advisable to forget the former, because one who does not observe them not only displeases but offends as well. Many times swords are drawn on account of this alone: one citizen, meeting another on the street, did not feel he was shown due deference.[32] For, as I have said, the force of custom is extraordinarily powerful and in such matters should be held as law. For this reason the man who addresses another man saying "Sir" doesn't give him a gift, unless the other is from a very low class. On the contrary, if he addressed him as "You" he would be detracting something from him, showing him disrespect and harm by using a word customarily used only for addressing good-for-nothings and peasants.[33] Although other nations and other centuries had different customs from ours in this regard, and since it would be pointless to discuss which of the two is better, it's advisable for us to obey not the good but the contemporary custom, just as we obey even laws which are less than good, until the Senate or whoever is in power makes changes. Thus, we must diligently assume the gestures and words which usage and modern custom dictate in the land we inhabit; normally they are employed in welcoming, greeting, and addressing each man according to his worth and so forth, among people we observe. The Admiral, when speaking with King

Peter of Aragon, many times addressed him as "thou," according to the custom of his times;[34] nevertheless in our age we address kings as "Your Majesty" and "Your Highness" both orally and in letters. In fact, just as he served the customs of his century, so we must not disobey ours. I call these ceremonies of duty, for they do not originate from our own desire or free will but are imposed upon us by law, that is, by general custom. In matters that do not have anything wicked about them, but rather seem to have an appearance of courtesy, one should—in fact it makes sense to—follow general customs and not to dispute or wrangle over them. Although to kiss as a sign of reverence is strictly suited only for relics of saints' bodies or other sacred things, nonetheless, if in your neighborhood it is the custom when leaving to say, "Sir, I kiss your hand" or "I am your servant" or even "I am your slave in chains," you must not be more reticent than others; rather when leaving or writing you must greet and say goodbye not according to reason but to how use wants you to, and not as one used to do or should do, but as one does in this day and age.[35] And you must not say "What is he a master of, anyway?" or "Has this man become my parish priest, that I should kiss his hand?" For the man who is accustomed to being called "sir" by others and similarly calls others "sir" will think you disdain him or are slandering him when you address him by his first name or as mister. As I've already told you, these words indicating position or service and others like them have lost their stiffness, having been so much in people's mouths, like some herbs left in water that turn to pulp and go mushy. One should not shun them, as do some rude clodhoppers who would rather have people begin their letters to emperors and kings in this manner: "If you and your kids are feeling well, I feel very well myself."[36] They claim that this was the salutation used by the ancient Latin orators when addressing letters to the Commune in Rome. If we were to go back to the past like this, little by little we would revert to living on acorns. But even in these compliments paid out of duty, so as not to appear to others arrogant or snobbish, we must obey certain norms. First of all, one must consider the country where one lives, for every custom is not good in every place. Perhaps what is customary for Neapolitans, whose city is rich in men of great lineage and barons of great prestige, would not do, for example, for the people of Lucca or Florentines who are for the most part merchants and simple gentlemen and have among them neither princes, nor counts, nor barons. Therefore, the stately and pompous manners of Naples transferred to Florence, like the clothes of a big man put on a little one, would be baggy and superfluous; to the nobility of Neapolitans and perhaps to their nature, neither more nor less than the manners of the Florentines would appear meager and skimpy. And just because the Venetian gentlemen compliment and flatter each other beyond compare on account of their many political posts and campaigns for election, it would not be fitting for the nobles of Rovigo or citizens of Asolo to maintain that same degree of solemnity in mutual reverence, all for nothing. All the countryside, unless I am mistaken, has gotten totally lost in this nonsense, perhaps because of indifference, or maybe having taken the lead from Venice, their lady, for everyone follows the footsteps of his master, without knowing why. In addition to that, you must respect the time, age, and status of those with whom you are using these formalities, and your own position. With men who have a lot to do we must completely eliminate formalities, or at least cut these as short as possible, and preferably nod tacitly and omit all empty phrases. The courtiers in Rome know how to do this perfectly. In other places, however, formalities are a great obstacle to business and are very tedious. "Put on your coat," says the harried judge in a rush for time; and the man before him first performs a number of bows, with much shuffling of feet, and then, speaking slowly, answers him: "My lord, I am fine as I am." But still the judge says, "Put on your coat." And so the man, bending two or three times to each side and bowing to the ground answers in a solemn voice: "I beseech your lordship to allow me to do my duty." And this skirmish continues so long and so much time is wasted that the judge could very nearly have dispatched his morning's business. Therefore, although it is every person's duty to honor judges and men of higher rank, when time does not permit, this regard to punctilio is tedious and must be either avoided or curtailed. It is not suitable for young men to use those same formalities among themselves that older men use; nor is it fitting for the lower classes or little people to use those that aristocrats affect. Men of real talent and great excellence do not use many formalities; nor do they appreciate or expect that many be used toward them, for they will not waste their thoughts on such vain matters. Neither should artisans and men of low sort be too concerned with using solemn compliments toward great men and lords; coming from them, these formalities would be irritating, since it is obedience rather than homage that is expected. For this reason the servant errs who makes too much a show of offering services to his master, for the master will be offended, thinking that the servant intends to place in doubt his master's superiority, almost as if he had no right to command and expect obedience. These kinds of ceremony should be performed liberally, so what one person does is received as payment for a debt, not an exaggeration on the part of the one who gives it. But he who offers much more than required seems to offer something of his own and so is loved and held to be magnificent. And I recall that a noble and great Greek poet used to say that he who knows how to caress people with words is able with little capital to reap some nice profits.[37] Therefore, you will handle formalities as the tailor does cloth; that is, cutting them larger rather than smaller, but not so much that when you want to make a pair of round hose you end up with a sack or a cloak. Therefore, if you use a suitable degree of largess toward your inferiors you will be considered courteous; and if you do the same toward your superiors you will be called a polite gentleman. But he who is overly lavish and squandering will be accused of being vain and fatuous, and, perhaps worse, it may happen that he will be considered evil and a flatterer and, as I hear some literary men say, a fawning parasite. It is a vice our ancients called, if I'm not mistaken, sycophancy; no sin is more abominable or unbecoming to a gentleman than this one. And this is the third kind of ceremony which arises from our own will and not from custom. Let us remember, therefore, that formalities, as I said from the start, are not necessary by nature. In fact, one could do without them, as our nation did until not so very long ago. But someone else's ills have sickened us with this and many other infirmities. For this reason, once we have obeyed custom and used such permissible lies, anything more is superfluous and a transparent, bold-faced lie; indeed it is impermissible and forbidden to go further than custom allows, because formalities then become a noisome and boring thing for men of noble spirit, who do not indulge in such ostentatious games and pretenses. You must know that when I was composing this present treatise, not trusting in my little knowledge, I sought out the opinions of worthier men of learning, and I found out that a king, whose name was Oedipus, having been banished from his own city, sought refuge at the court of Theseus, king of Athens, for his enemies were pursuing him. As he was about to present himself to the king, Oedipus heard one of his daughters speak and, recognizing her voice, for he was blind, did not extend his greetings to Theseus but, as a father would, embraced the girl. Realizing, then, his error, he wanted to apologize to the king and ask forgiveness. However, the good and wise Theseus would not allow him to speak but instead said: "Take heart, it's not through words but actions that I want to set the luster on my life."[38] One must keep this sentence in mind. Although men greatly like to be respected by others, nevertheless when they are aware that they are being honored for the sake of mere formality they grow weary; moreover, they disdain it because flattery, or I should say adulation, besides being evil and repulsive, has this additional fault: flatterers overtly show that they consider the man they are praising to be vain and arrogant, as well as so stupid, obtuse, and so beef-witted that it is easy to lure and entrap him. Empty, elaborate, and excessive formalities are but thinly disguised adulation. In fact, everybody clearly sees them and recognizes them as such, so that those who employ them for their own advantage, in addition to being evil as I said above, are also unpleasant and plain annoying.

17

Why imported Spanish affectation is particularly vapid

There is another kind of ceremonious person, the kind who makes an art and a business of it, and who wrote the book on the subject. To one person, they scowl or grimace, to another instead lend a smile; to the higher-class person they will offer the comfortable chair, while putting the low-class person on a wooden bench. I believe such affected ceremonies have been brought into Italy from Spain, but our land has received them badly and hardly is set up for them, and no one in Italy makes such precious distinctions between degrees of social class, and, therefore, no one must stand in judgment as to who is ranked more or less noble. Nor should kindnesses and praises be sold, as they are by strumpets. This I have seen many men do in their courts, who hand out compliments to their unfortunate servants instead of giving them a decent wage. And surely whoever takes pleasure in using formalities so far beyond the circumstances does so out of pettiness and conceit, like men of little weight. Because such idle compliments are so easily displayed and make a bit of a good show, these men learn it through study. They cannot comprehend more grave matters, being too weak for such a burden, and not knowing anything better, they would prefer that all conversation be spent on these frivolities. And beneath that glossy skin, these fruits have no juice and when touched are all rotten and moldy. For this reason they would love all dealings with people to not proceed beyond first impressions. And you are going to find there are an enormous number of such people. There are others who abound in words and courteous deeds only to make up for their own ignorance and for their mean, villainous, and stingy souls; they are aware that if they were as barren and brutish in words as they are in accomplishments, they would be insufferable. And surely you are going to find that for one of these two reasons, and for none other, the majority of people abound in superfluous formalities, which generally irritate the mass of men, keeping them from living as they see fit and impeding their liberty, which is what one desires above everything.

18

Other spoken sources of annoyance: slander, contradiction, reprimanding, etc.

One should not speak ill either of other men or of their affairs, even if it's clear that we gladly lend an ear to such talk, envious as we are of others' possessions and honor. But in the end everyone flees the charging bull, and men eschew the friendship of those bad-mouthers, figuring that what they tell us of others they could also tell others of us. And those who contradict every word and always question and dispute show how little they know of the nature of men, that everyone loves victory and hates being defeated in discussion as well as in action: it goes without saying that contradicting others is the work of enmity, not of friendship. For this reason whoever loves being friendly and sweet in conversation must not have a ready

"It's not like that" or "Say what you like, but I am right about this," nor place bets on every trifle. Instead, he must make an effort to be conciliatory to others in those matters that are of little account. Victory in such cases turns to our detriment, for in winning a point in a frivolous debate he will often lose some cherished friend; he becomes so maddening to others that they dare not try to stay on friendly terms, so as to escape constant squabbling. And they nickname such ones "Mister Know-it-all," or "Sir Counterpoint," or "Sir Expert," and in old times "the Subtle Doctor."[39] Although it may sometimes happen that one is invited into disputes by these types, one must engage sweetly and without that thirst for the sweetness of victory that will make the other man choke. Instead, it is proper to let everyone play his part and, whether the opponent is right or wrong, to abide by the majority opinion or by the more importunate, and then leave the field of battle to them, so that others and not you will be the ones to debate, sweat, and get worn out. These are unseemly occupations not suited to well-behaved men, and so procure hatred and dislike. Furthermore, such men are unpleasant because they are unseemly and thus an annoyance to those with well-disposed minds, as I might explore a little later on. Most people, however, are so infatuated with themselves that they overlook other people's pleasures; and in order to show themselves to be subtle, intuitive, and sagacious, they will advise, and correct, and argue, and contradict vigorously, not agreeing with anything except their own opinions. To offer your advice without having been asked is nothing else but a way of saying that you are wiser than those you are giving advice, and even a reproof for their ignorance and lack of knowledge. For this reason, this should not be done with everyone you know, but only with your best and closest friends and with people who depend on your guidance, or with a stranger who happens to be in great and imminent danger. In daily matters, however, one must abstain both from giving advice and from compensating for other's shortcomings. Many fall into these errors and most often it is the least intelligent, because slow-witted men have little on their minds and so do not spend time in reaching a decision, like those who do not have many alternatives available to them. Whatever the case, whoever goes about offering and disseminating advice shows himself of the opinion that he has more wisdom than he needs, and that others lack it. And there are some who are so highly conceited with their own wisdom that not following their advice is tantamount to coming to blows with them, and they say, "That's fine, a simple man's advice is never taken"; "So-and-so will do whatever he wants"; and "Of course, they won't listen to me." As if demanding that others obey your counsel did not show greater arrogance than wanting to follow only your own. A sin similar to this is committed by those who take it upon themselves to correct other men's failings and reprimand them, and want to pass final judgment upon everything; and to everyone they lay down the law. "You really shouldn't have done that"; and "That was certainly not a nice thing to say"; and "The wine you drink is not healthy for you. You should drink only red wine"; and "You should really be taking some herbal syrup and some pills." And they never finish their reprimanding or criticizing. Not only do they tend to busy themselves in weeding someone else's garden while their own grows full of crabgrass and nettles, but they are too much a pain to notice. Just as there are few or none who could suffer to live with a doctor or confessor, much less with a criminal court justice, so, likewise, there are few to be found who will risk becoming friendly with these types; simply put, everyone loves freedom, and by appearing to be our teachers they deprive us of it. For this reason it is not a pleasant habit to be so desirous of correcting and teaching others. This must be left to teachers and fathers from whom, as you well know, sons and students are eager to flee.

19

The risks of mockery and
ridicule and vituperative wit

One should never mock a person, no matter how much he is an enemy, for it seems that ridicule shows greater contempt than injury. A man wrongs another out of resentment or covetousness, and no one is upset by something that he esteems worthless or desires something which he despises completely. So one has already little esteem for the man one injures, but for the man one mocks, none at all or very little. Mocking consists in our taking delight in humiliating others, with no benefit for us. Therefore, it is good manners to refrain from mocking anyone. They behave badly who reprove others for some defect either with words, as Messer Forese da Rabatta did when he scoffed at Master Giotto's appearance,[40] or with actions, as many do, mimicking those who stutter, or limp, or are hunchbacked. Likewise it is unacceptable to laugh at people who are deformed, misshapen, scrawny, or dwarfish; or to chuckle and rejoice over an idiotic thing someone said; or to take pleasure in making others blush. Such spiteful ways deserve to be detested. Very similar to these are those buffoons who enjoy playing tricks and teasing, not because they want to scorn or deride, but simply for the fun of it. Know that there is no difference between joking and mocking except in purpose and intention; for joking is done for amusement, and mocking is done to harm, while in common parlance these two words are often interchanged: but whoever mocks is happy with the embarrassment of another, while he who jokes is not satisfied but rather amused by another's error, and if the other man were ashamed, the joker would feel pained and sad. Although in my childhood I did not progress very far in grammar school, I can still remember how Micio, who loved Aeschinus so much that he was amazed by it, did nevertheless take pleasure in making fun of him, as when he said to himself: "Cur non ludo hunc aliquantisper."[41] And so the same thing done to the same person, depending only on intention, will be either laughing with someone or laughing at someone. Since our intention is not easily clear to others, it is not fitting to indulge in practices so dubious and suspect, and one should avoid them rather than seek to be considered a prankster; just as it often happens in games and in sports that one man smacks another as a joke and the other receives it as the start of a brawl and thus fun turns into a scrap, so the man who is mocked by a friend will sometimes interpret it as an insult to his honor and take umbrage. Not to mention that a joke is a deception, and everyone naturally dislikes being wrong and being duped. It then follows for many reasons that whoever seeks to be well liked and held dear should not make himself a master of merry pranks. It is true that we cannot lead this weary mortal life of ours without any recreation or any rest whatsoever, and since jests do create some fun and laughter and therefore recreation, we like people who are funny, entertaining, and easy-going. For this reason the opposite would seem true, that is, that it makes sense to sometimes crack a joke and be facetious. And certainly those who know how to joke in a friendly and pleasant manner are better liked than those who cannot or don't know how. But it is necessary to keep in mind many things: since the intention of the joker is to make fun of an error in someone he respects, the error committed must be such that no noticeable shame or serious harm could arise from it; otherwise it would be hard to distinguish quips from slander. There are also persons who are so embittered that one should under no circumstance poke fun at them, as Biondello found out from Mr. Filippo Argenti in the Loggia de' Cavicciuli.[42] Similarly, one must not make jokes about either solemn or shameful matters. According to the proverb of the simple people, it makes evil seem like a joke, although Madonna Filippa da Prato did this to her advantage with witty retorts she gave when questioned about her infidelity.[43] This is why, in my opinion, Lupo degli Uberti did not soften his shame but rather aggravated it, when with a wisecrack he excused himself for his wickedness and cowardice. Though he could have held the castle of Laterina, he gave it up instead; and seeing it besieged and finding himself trapped inside, he said that wolves are not used to being locked up.[44] Where there is no place for laughter, there is no room for puns and prattle.

20

Comic talent: those who are funny and those who try to be

You must also know that there is some wit that bites and some that does not bite. Of the former it is enough that you abide by Lauretta's sage advice: that is, witty sayings should bite the hearer as a sheep does rather than as a dog does; if it bit like a dog it would not be wit but abuse. In nearly every city, law dictates that whoever slanders someone else should be severely punished, and perhaps one should also have ordained no light penalty for anyone using biting jokes toward others beyond measure.[45] But polite men should consider that the law against slander extends to humor as well, and therefore poke fun at someone else only rarely and gingerly. Besides all this, you must realize that unless a joke, whether biting or toothless, is pleasant and subtle, those who hear it will take no delight; rather, they will be bored by it, or if they laugh, they laugh at the teller and not the wit. Bons mots are nothing else but deceptions, and deceptions, being subtle and sly, must be carried out only by astute men with a ready wit and, above all, capable of improvising. Therefore, they are not suitable to stolid individuals with dull intellects, nor to anyone whose wit is abundant and good, as they perhaps did not befit Giovanni Boccaccio very well. Witty remarks require a special poise and charm, and immediate mental alacrity. For this reason sensible men do not pay attention to their wishes but to their aptitude; having tried once or twice the force of their humor in vain— and realizing that they have no gifts for humor—they give up the sham, fearing to face what happened to the knight of Madonna Oretta.[46] And if you will put your mind to the manners of the multitudes, you will easily recognize that what I am saying is true; that it is not good that whoever wants to be amusing should try to be, but only those who are able. You will see that some men attach each word with one, no, with more of those inane jests we call puns, or switch syllables around within a word in frivolous or dumb ways; or answer in a manner people were never expecting, and with no ingenuity or charm, such as: "Where is he? Where his feet are," and "He greased his palms with the oil of John Boccadoro," and "Where are you sending me? To the Arno," or "I want to shave. It would be better not to shove."[47] These, as you can very easily see, are cheap, low-class jokes, fit only for clowns and porters. Such were, for the most part, the pleasantries and puns used by Dioneo.[48] Our task at the moment is not to discuss which jokes and witticisms are more or less elegant, for there are other treatises on this,[49] written by far better writers and experts than I; and witticisms have broad and sure proofs of their beauty or of their unpleasantness; and so you will not easily go wrong unless you are overly dazzled by yourself. Where a pleasant witticism has been said, there immediately is joy, laughter, and a kind of astonishment. Where your pleasantries are not rewarded with the laughter of listeners, cease and desist from telling jokes in the future. The defect is in you, not in your listeners, who are tickled by charming or quick or subtle quips and retorts, and even if they try they cannot hold back their laughter and laugh despite themselves. They are like a lawful and just jury against whose judgment you must not appeal in your own defense or try repeatedly to prove your worth. One should not, for the sake of making someone laugh, say obscene words or indulge in such vile or perverse acts as distorting one's face and eyes or gesticulating like a dope, for no one should debase himself in order to amuse others. This is the habit not of a gentleman but of slapstick actors and professional buffoons. So don't imitate that vulgar, plebeian language of Dioneo: "Monna Aldruda, come, lift up your tail."[50] Nor act like a lunatic or a numbskull, but if possible say at the proper time something clever and new, something no one else has thought of, or else keep quiet. For these are movements of the mind, and if they are pleasant and lively, they are an indication and a testimonial of the nimble mind and the good habits of the speaker—this is particularly liked by other men and endears us to them. But if they are without grace and charm, they have the contrary effect, so it appears a jackass is joking, or that someone very fat with an enormous butt is dancing and hopping about in a tight-fitting vest.

21

Some practical tips on storytelling

There is another entertaining way of speaking: that is, when the pleasure lies not in jokes and funny anecdotes, which are generally brief, but in an extended, continuous tale. This must be well arranged, properly expressed, and reflect the manners, customs, gestures, and habits of those one is speaking to, so they will believe not that they are hearing a story but that they are seeing with their own eyes what you narrate. Boccaccio's men and women knew very well how to do this, though sometimes, if I'm not mistaken, they impersonated the characters more than is suitable for ladies and gentlemen, more like those comic actors in plays. In order to do this, you must have in your mind the anecdote, or story, or event that you picked to narrate all thought through, with the words all laid out and ready so that you will not be required to say every so often: "That thing"; and "That man"; or "What's his name?" or "That stuff about"; or "How should I put it"; and "What did I say his name was?" This was precisely the plodding gait of Madonna Oretta's knight. If you narrate an event in which many men took part, you must not say "That one said" and "This one answered," for "this" could be any one, and so the listener could easily misunderstand; thus, the storyteller must give the names and not confuse them later. Furthermore, one should be careful not to say things that left out would make the story no less enjoyable, and perhaps even more so. "So-and-so, who was the son of the man who lived in Via del Cocomero,[51] you know him, don't you? His wife was one of the Gianfigliazzi girls. A kind of skinny girl who used to go to Mass at San Lorenzo. What do you mean you don't know her? Of course, you knew him. A tall old man, with long hair down on his shoulders, don't you remember him?" If it did not matter whether the event happened to this man or to another, all this long disquisition would be to no purpose, indeed very tedious to the listeners, who are desirous and impatient to hear the end of the story you began. You would make the listener wait, as it so happened our Dante did:

My parents were from Lombardy--
Mantua was their homeland.[52]

Indeed, it would make no difference if his mother had been from Gazzuolo, or even from Cremona.[53] In fact, I received from a great foreign rhetorician a very useful recommendation about this, and that is that stories should be thought out and ordered first using nicknames, and then narrated using real names, for the former are given according to a person's character while the latter are given according to the father's pleasure or some other such authority. And so that character whom you were thinking of as Mr. Stingy in your narration will become Mr. Erminio Grimaldi, if the general opinion your neighbors have of him is the same as was said of Mr. Erminio to Guglielmo Borsieri in Genoa.[54] If in your city there is not a person similarly well known that would suit your need, you must imagine the story unfolding in another city and then give the man whatever name you like. It is certainly true that one listens with more pleasure and keener imagination to stories that involve people known to us—given that the event is suited to their manners—than to stories about strangers. The reason for this is obvious: knowing that a certain person tends to act in a particular way, we assume he has acted accordingly and we see it, while with strangers this does not happen.

22

Eloquence and the choice of language

Both in polite conversation and in other types of speech, words must be clear enough that everyone listening can easily understand them, and equally beautiful in sound and in sense. And so if you must choose one of these two words, you will rather say "stomach" than "abdomen," and where your language will bear it you will rather say "belly" instead of "guts" or "body" and thus you will be understood, not misunderstood, as the Florentines say, and you will not bring to your audience anything unpleasant or obscene. Wanting to avoid such implications in this very word, I believe your most excellent poet sought another with paraphrase. And he said:

Remember that it was our sin made God
take on, for our salvation,
the flesh of man in your virginal cloister.[55]

And since Dante, also a supreme poet, did not pay much attention to such precepts, so I find that little good can be said of him in this regard. Certainly I would not advise you to make him your teacher in this art of being elegant, since he himself was not. In fact, in some chronicle I find this written about him: "On account of his knowledge, Dante was presumptuous, scornful, and disdainful; and lacking in grace, as philosophers are, he did not know very well how to converse with laymen."[56] But returning to our discussion, I say that words ought to be clear; this will be the case if you know how to choose those that are native to your region, and not so antiquated that they have become rancid and corrupt and, like worn-out clothes, laid aside and out of use: *spaldo* and *epa* and *uopo* and *sezzaio* and *primaio*.[57] Furthermore, the words you have at hand should not have double meanings, but one only; for by combining ambiguous words one creates that kind of speech which is called doubletalk or, in simple terms, gibberish:

I saw a man
Pass from both sides
With seven strides.[58]

Words should also be as much as possible appropriate to what you want to show, and as little applicable to other things; thus, it will seem that you are bringing forth the very things being described, not with words, but as if held in your fingers. Therefore it is preferable to say that a man is "recognized by his features" rather than "by his shape" or "by his looks." Dante represented what he was saying when he said,

they're so dense,
like scales we creak beneath their weight,[59]

better than if he had said either "shouted," "screeched," or "made noise." It is more precise to say "the shivers of quartan fever" than "a cold"; and "this fatty, gristly meat makes one feel nauseous" rather than "I'm full"; and "hang out the laundry to dry" rather than "spread it out"; and "stumps" rather than "cut-off limbs"; and

And just as in a ditch at water's edge,
frogs squat with but their snouts in sight,[60]

rather than "with their mouths." These are all words that have one meaning only. And similarly we should say the "hem of a piece of cloth," rather than "the edge." Well I know that if, as my bad luck would have it, a foreigner came across this treatise of mine, he would mock me and say that I was teaching you how to speak in slang or in ciphers, since these words are, for the most part, particular to the Tuscan region and no other nation uses them, and if used they would not be understood. And who is there who knows what Dante meant in this, "No cask ever gapes so wide for loss"?[61]

I certainly doubt anyone but us Florentines. Nevertheless,

so I've been told, if there is any fault in Dante's text, it does not lie in the words. If he erred, he erred rather in that he, being rather antisocial, undertook to speak of something uneasily captured in words and so unpleasant to hear, not because he could not express himself. Therefore, no one can converse effectively with someone who does not understand the idiom being spoken. If a German does not understand Latin, we must not ruin our own speech when communicating with him, nor engage in mimicry like Master Brufaldo, as some people do, who stupidly force themselves to speak in the language of the person they are speaking to, whatever it may be, and say everything backward.[62] It often happens that the Spaniard will speak Italian with an Italian, and the Italian, to show off and to be pompous, will talk to him in Spanish, and yet it is easier to realize that they are both conversing in a foreign tongue than to keep from laughing at the new fustian that comes out of their mouths. We shall communicate then in a foreign language only when necessary in order to express our needs; but in common use let us continue to speak our own language, even if inferior, rather than another, superior one. For a Lombard will speak more properly in his own dialect, though it is the weirdest, than he would in Tuscan or any other because he will never have easily at hand, try as he might, the proper and precise words that you Tuscans know. And if anyone, in order to show consideration for the people he is speaking with, seeks to avoid using the regional diction, which I mentioned, and instead uses generic, standard words, his conversation will thus become considerably less pleasant. Every gentleman in addition must also avoid saying obscene, unpleasant words. Decency in words depends on their sound, or their pronunciation, or on their meaning. Some words signify a decent thing, yet all the same in pronouncing them we hear something crude, such as *rinculare*, which is nevertheless used every day by everyone, but if any person, man or woman, were to use some word to signify "to do yourself in front" coined in the same manner as that word for "move back," then obviously the word would sound offensive: but in parlance we sense almost the wine of this word, rather than the sediment.[63] "The thief raised up his fists and cried," your Dante once said, but your women do not dare to put it like that.[64] In fact, in order to avoid that lewd word they prefer to say *le castagne* instead; often some women will say without thinking that which, if others said it so casually, would make them turn red in the face, since then it describes that which makes them females. Therefore, let those ladies who are or want to be well-mannered take care to avoid not only indecent things but also offensive words, and not only those that definitely are but also those that could be or could appear to be indecent, vulgar, or coarse, as some say those used by Dante are;

the wind in my face and blowing from below[65]

or else these:

Tell us, then, where is the nearest opening:
Follow us and you shall find the gap.[66]

You must realize that though two or more words could mean the same thing, nonetheless one will be more, the other less, decent. And so one should say, "She spent the night with him" or "she satisfied him with her body," because this idea, said with other words, would be obscene to hear. It would be more polite for you to call one "my sweetheart" rather than "my amorous paramour," even though both these words mean "lover." It seems to be a more acceptable manner of speech to say "my girl" or "my lady friend" rather than "my concubine of Tithonus." It is more mannerly for a lady and even for a gentleman to call prostitutes streetwalkers, as Monna Belcolore, more shameful in her speech than in her actions, did, rather than to adopt their common name: "She is Thaïs, the whore."[67] And, as Boccaccio said, "the power of whores and boys"; it would have been vulgar and shameful if he had used a term for the boys as he had for the women based on their occupation.[68] In fact, one should refrain not only from indecent and obscene words but also from vile words, especially where one speaks of high and noble matters. For this reason, perhaps, Beatrice deserved some blame when she said:

> Broken would be the high decree of God
> should Lethe be crossed and its sustenance
> be tasted without payment of some fee:
> his penitence that shows itself in tears.[69]

In my opinion, the base word appropriate in a tavern did not fit in such a noble discussion. Nor should one say "lamp of the world" in place of "the sun" because for some persons such an expression implies the stink of oil and of the kitchen. Nor would any prudent man say that Saint Dominic was "the amorous lover"[70] of Theology, nor would he say that the glorious saints had uttered such base words as:

> and then let him who itches scratch,[71]

which are sullied with the filth of the masses, as anyone can tell.

Therefore, when you speak at length you must attend to the considerations above and others which you may easily learn from your teachers and from that art called rhetoric. In other kinds of speech you must accustom yourself to using words that are polite, simple, and sweet, so that there is in your language no bitter flavor. You will sooner say, "I'm not sure how to say it" than "You don't understand what I'm saying"; and "Let's just consider if it is really so, as we are saying," rather than "You're completely wrong" or "That's just not true. You don't know what you're talking about." It's a polite and pleasant habit to excuse a man's fault even when you know him to be in the wrong. In fact, one should share a friend's mistake and first claim a portion of the blame, and then reprove him for it and fix it. You should say, "We've taken a wrong turn," and "Yesterday we did not remember to do such and such," although it was your friend alone who was absentminded, not you. What Restagnone said to his companions was not right— "If your words are not lies"[72]—because it's extremely impolite to impugn a person's veracity. In fact, if someone promises you something and does not deliver, it is not correct for you to say, "You did not keep your word," unless you are forced to say it by some necessity, protecting your own honor, for instance. If someone has deceived you, you should sooner say, "You did not know what you were doing," and if he did not remember something you should say, "It probably slipped your mind," rather than "You forgot?" or "I guess you couldn't even bother to keep your promise you made to me." Such words have in them the sting of spite and the poison of provocation; because of this, those who make a habit of using such words are considered morose and rough, and one shuns their company as much as one avoids becoming caught in a briar patch.

<h1 style="text-align:center">23</h1>

More on the fine art of conversation

I've known some people who have that nasty and unpleasant habit of being so ambitious and eager to speak that they miss the point; instead, they run right past it like a hound never able to catch his prey. I am going to tell you something that may seem totally unnecessary, since it is so manifestly true: you must never speak unless you have first formed in your mind what you have to say. In this way your speech will be brought to birth and not miscarry—any stranger happening to read this screed of mine will permit me to use this word. If you don't make light of my instruction, you will never find yourself caught saying, "Come right in, Mr. Agostino," to someone whose name is actually Agnolo or Bernardo; and you will not be forced to say, "Remind me, what was your name again," or say over and over again, "I'm not putting it very well," nor "Gosh, how can I say it," nor stammer nor stutter at length in order to remember some word: "Mr. Arrigo, no, Mr. Arabico. What am I saying? Mr. Agapito!" Listening to this is like being stretched out on the rack. One's voice should be neither hoarse nor sharp. One should not squeak like a pulley wheel, neither with laughter nor for any other reason. Nor should someone speak while yawning. You know very well that we cannot acquire a silver tongue or a good voice at will, so anyone who squawks or croaks should not always be chattering away. Instead, he should correct the defect of his tongue through silence and with his ears, and he can also correct this defect of nature by practice. It is not proper to raise one's voice like a town crier, nor should one speak so softly that the listener cannot hear. If at first you have not been heard, you must not speak even more softly the second time around, nor should you shout so as to show that you are becoming irritated at having to repeat again what you have already said. Words must be arranged according to the demands of common speech, not confused and convoluted here and there, as with many haphazard speakers. The speech of these people is more like that of a notary translating into Italian the documents he dictated in Latin, rather than that of a man conversing in his vernacular. To say things such as, "pursuing those false images of good,"[73] and "my temples flower white before their time,"[74] may sometimes be suitable for someone writing poetry, but is always to be avoided when talking. In speaking, a man should avoid sounding like he is writing verses and also avoid the pomposity of a public speaker. Otherwise, he will be unpleasant and tedious to hear, even though a sermon may require more effort than conversation does. There is a time and a place for everything. A man on the street should walk, not dance, even though everyone knows how to walk but not everyone knows how to dance—dancing is for weddings, not for the streets. You will therefore avoid inflated speech such as: "It is believed by many philosophers" as well as the entire *Filoloco* and the other treatises by your Giovanni Boccaccio, except for the *Decameron* and, perhaps even more than that one, the *Corbaccio*. Nor yet would I have you become accustomed to the vulgar speech of the dregs of society, the washerwoman or the fruit vendor, but to that of gentlemen. I have shown you above how this can be done in part, that is, you must not speak of low things, or things frivolous, gross, or abominable. You must know how to choose among the words in your language the purest and most appropriate and those with the best sound and sense, without the insinuation of anything ugly, dirty, or low, and put them together without piling them up randomly or stringing them together with too much heady precision. And besides this you must seek to arrange your thoughts with discretion and avoid joining incompatible things, such as:

Cicero, Linus, and moral Seneca,[75]

or else

One was a Paduan, the other a layman.[76]

You must not speak slowly, like the person without will or appetite, nor hungrily as if you were starving; but you must speak as a moderate man should. You must pronounce sounds and syllables with a suitable grace, not like a schoolmaster teaching reading and writing to children. Nor should you chew your words, or swallow them all smashed and stuck together, one with the other. If you will keep in mind these and other similar lessons, people will listen to you eagerly and with pleasure, and you will maintain the rank and the dignity one expects from a properly raised and polite gentleman.

24

The verbose, the interrupters, the taciturn

There are moreover many people who cannot stop talking. Just as a ship driven by its force does not slow up when the sails are furled, so these people transported by a certain impetus run on and, having exhausted their ideas, still do not stop there; instead, they say again things already said and speak into thin air. Others are so avid to speak that they do not let others get a word in edgewise. Just as we sometimes see in a farmer's coop a chicken snatching grain from another's beak, so these men take the ideas out of the mouth of the man who began them, and then they start talking. They surely make the other person eager to punch or smack them; if you look carefully, nothing moves a man to fury more quickly than when his desire and pleasure is suddenly ruined, even if trivial. As if you just opened your mouth to yawn and someone covers it up with his hand, or when someone suddenly holds your arm from behind just when you raised it to hurl a stone. Therefore, just as these and many other similar behaviors tend to impede others' wishes and pleasures, and are unpleasant and ought to be avoided, even if done as a joke or for sport, so in speaking one should satisfy rather than impede other people's desires. Therefore, if someone is ready to tell a story, it is not suitable to ruin it for him, nor say you have already heard it. And if he inserts some fib in his story, he should not be chastised for it in words or in actions, such as shaking one's head or giving him a disparaging look, as people often do, who pretend they cannot bear under any circumstance the bitterness of a falsehood. This is seldom the real cause but rather the acrimony and sourness of their own rough and quarrelsome nature that renders them so spiteful and petty in the company of others that no one can stand them. Similarly, to interrupt someone as he is speaking is an importunate and irritating habit, not unlike that of holding back a man who is ready to run. Nor is it suitable to leave or ignore a man when he is speaking, or to point out to his listeners something else, or lead their attention to somewhere else: for it is not proper for anyone to dismiss a person whom others, not he, invited. You should pay attention to someone speaking, so that you will not have to say, again and again: "Huh?" or "What?" Many people labor under this fault, and it is no less a nuisance to a speaker than, if walking, he were every moment to trip over a stone. All these habits and generally all those which check or interfere with the course of words of another man are to be avoided. If anyone is slow in his speech, one should not get ahead of him or lend him words, as if you had a surplus and he was caught a bit short. Many people get offended by this, especially those who have persuaded themselves that they are good speakers; for then they believe that you do not have the same opinion of them as they hold of themselves and that you want to assist them at their own talent, much as merchants bristle if others offer to lend them money, as if they did not have enough themselves and were poor and in need of others' charity. You must realize that everyone believes he can speak well, even though some out of modesty deny it. I cannot guess why this is so, but those who know the least speak the most. Courteous men should guard themselves against this, that is, against being verbose, especially if they know little, not only because it is remarkable if one can speak a lot without making many mistakes, but also because it seems that he who is speaking stands in a certain way above the listeners, like a master over his disciples. Therefore, appropriating a greater portion of superiority than befits a person is bad practice. Not only do many men fall into this sin, but also many chattering and babbling nations, and woe be to the ears they seize upon. Just as speaking too much is a nuisance, so keeping too silent is despicable, for to be taciturn where others are engaged in conversation seems to show unwillingness to foot one's share of the bill. Because speaking is a way of opening your soul to your listener, to affect a haughty silence seems to imply, on the contrary, a willingness to remain an unknown. For this reason, just as in some countries where people drink a lot at their feasts and get drunk it is the custom to throw out those who do not drink, so this type of mute is not eagerly welcomed in cheerful, friendly company. It is a pleasant habit, therefore, for each to speak and to stay quiet when his turn comes.

25

Anecdote of the sculptor, *The Rule*, and a lady named Reason

According to a very ancient chronicle, there once lived in Morea a good man, a sculptor by trade, who was so clear-headed that he was called, I believe, Chiarissimo.[77] Because he was already well up in years, this man wrote a treatise in which he gathered up all the rules of his craft with the authority of someone who knows his art. He demonstrated how the limbs of the human body ought to be measured, each by itself and each in relation to the others so that they should be in proper proportion. He called this volume *The Rule,* meaning that henceforth every master of the craft should shape and design statues according to it, just as beams, stones, and walls are measured with a standard ruler. But the fact is that it's much easier to talk about things than to make or create them. And most men, and especially we laymen and uneducated types, are always readier with the senses than with the intellect; therefore, we learn better through simple things and specific examples than through general principles and syllogisms, which in the common parlance means reasons. In order to demonstrate even more clearly his own expertise, the above-mentioned valiant man, aware as he was of the lack of talent, acquired a fine block of marble, from which, after long and difficult labor, he carved a statue proportioned in limbs and symmetrical in parts as his treatise recommended. And, just like the book, he called the statue *The Rule.* Now, God willing, I will do, dearest child, at least in part, one of the two things that this noble sculptor and teacher knew how to do perfectly: that is, to put together in this volume the proper measures of the art I treat! It is too late for me to fulfill the other part and actually compose the second "rule," to live and display in my behavior the above-mentioned regulations, making of them a visible example, like the actual statue. This is so because in matters dealing with manners and customs of men, it is not enough to know the science and the rules, but necessary to put them into effect through use. This cannot be acquired in a moment or in a short span of time, but this must be done over many, many years. And, as you see, I have only a few years left. But for this you should not place less faith in these teachings: a man can well direct others to follow that road on which he took many wrong turns; those who lose their way, in fact, can perhaps remember better the misleading paths and doubts than one who takes only the right route. If those who took care of me in childhood, when we are tender and impressionable, had known how to bend my habits, maybe somewhat hard and coarse by nature, and how to soften and polish them, I could probably have become the man I am now trying to make of you. Although the forces of nature are great, nevertheless they are often won over and corrected by custom. But it is necessary to begin to resist them early, to rein them in before they take on too much power and boldness. Most people don't do this but instead are misled by their instincts, following them without opposition wherever they may lead. They believe themselves obeying nature, almost as if reason were not in man a natural thing. On the contrary, reason is a lady and a teacher: she has the power to change corrupt habits and assist and lift up nature whenever, from time to time, it stoops or falls. We do not listen to her, most of the time, and so are similar to those whom God did not grant reason, to the beasts. Yet reason has some power over these animals; not their own reason, for they have none, but ours. This you can see in horses that often, in fact always, would remain by nature wild, if their tamer did not render them meek, and in addition to that nearly erudite and well-behaved. For although many such animals would proceed in a hard trot, he teaches them to proceed with a light step, to stay, to run, to turn, and to jump. And they learn it, as you know they do. Now, if horses, dogs, birds, and many other animals still more proud than these submit to someone else's reason, and obey, and learn that which they did not know—what they revolted against—and become nearly virtuous and sensible, to the extent that their condition allows it, how much better, one imagines, would we become if taught by reason, if we would just lend her an ear? But the senses love and lust for immediate delights, whatever they may be, and they abhor bothersome things and put them off, and so they avoid reason as well, which seems bitter to them. Reason often presents them not with pleasure, which is often poisonous, but with their own good, which always requires an effort and tastes bitter to the still corrupted taste buds. Thus, while we still live according to the senses we are like the poor invalid to whom every dish, no matter how delicate and luscious, seems sour and salty, who then complains about the servant girl or the cook, who is not to blame at all, for in fact the sick one tastes his own bitterness, in that his tongue has twisted back on itself, and not the food. Thus reason, which is in itself so sweet, seems to us bitter because of our flavor, not its own. Being delicate and spoiled, we therefore refuse to taste it, covering again our vice with the cliché about there being no spur or rein that can change nature, drive her on or hold her back. Certainly if bulls or donkeys or maybe pigs could talk, I believe, they would not proffer a thought fouler or more depraved than this one. We would only be children in our mature years and in our old age, and we would still be romping like toddlers, were it not for reason, which grows in us with our years. And, once grown up, she renders from near-beasts, men. Thus, she has powerful force over the senses and the instincts, and it is our wickedness, not her fault, if we trespass in our lives and in our habits. It is therefore not true that against nature there is neither rein nor master. On the contrary, there are two of them, one being good manners, the other reason. But, as I have just said, reason cannot make the uncouth debonair without experience, which is part and parcel of time. Consequently, one should begin to listen to reason early on, not only because a man has more time to become accustomed to be as she teaches and to become her friend and belong to her, but also because youth, being pure, can be dyed every color, and also because those things one first grew accustomed to will always please the most. And for this reason we say that Theodorus, a great master in reciting comedies, always wanted his own play staged first, even if those who were to appear before him were not highly esteemed: he did not want his voice to reach the ears of spectators used to other sounds, however much inferior to his own.[78] Since, for the reasons I have told you, I cannot suit my deeds to my words as did the teacher Chiarissimo—who could do and could teach—let it suffice for me to have said, at least in part, that which one should do, even if I am unfit to put any part of it into practice. But just as in seeing darkness one learns what light is, and in silence one learns what sound would be, so also you will be able to perceive, in looking at my dark and hardly appealing ways, what the light of pleasant and praiseworthy manners may be. Returning to the analysis, which will shortly come to a close, let us say that pleasant manners are those which delight or at least do not annoy any of the senses, the desires, or the imagination of those with whom we live. This is what we have been talking about till now.

26

The aesthetics of human language and human actions

You must also recognize that men are very fond of beauty, symmetry, and proportion; and, on the contrary, men detest things that are ugly, monstrous, and deformed: this is our special privilege, for the other animals cannot understand any degree of beauty or proportion. And as things which we do not share with beasts but are really ours, we must appreciate them and hold them very dear, and those who have greater sensibility are all the more capable of understanding them. And although it is hard to express precisely what beauty is, so that you may have some indication of it, I want you to know this: where there is an appropriate measure among the parts in themselves and proportion between the parts and the whole, there beauty lies. And of something truly beautiful one can say it has proper measure. And from what I learned from a wise and educated man, the beautiful has as much unity as possible, while ugliness shows, on the contrary, multiplicity. Such are the faces of pretty, young girls, for their features appear to have been created for one unique face. This does not happen in the case of an ugly girl, for if she happens to have very large and bulging eyes, a tiny nose, chubby cheeks, thin lips, a protruding chin, or dark skin and blond hair, it seems that her face does not belong to one single woman but is composed from the faces of many people and made from pieces: some women can be found with different body parts which, regarded one at a time, can be really beautiful to the eye, but put together unpleasant and grotesque, simply because they are the features of several attractive women, and not of this one. She seems to have borrowed them from this girl or that. Perhaps that painter[79] who surrounded himself with nude girls from Calabria did nothing more than recognize in their parts what they had taken from one original female body. Once each girl had returned her borrowed limb to the original, he imagined her to possess so proportioned the beauty of Venus. I do not want you to think that this is true only for bodies and faces; in fact, it is just as applicable to speech and behavior, neither more nor less. If you saw an adorned noblewoman washing her dishes in a stream along the public street, you would be disappointed with her inconsistency, even if you did not otherwise care for her. Her appearance would be that of an elegant noble lady, but her behavior would be that of a low, servile woman. Even if there were no harsh odor or air about her, nor any displeasing sound or color, nor anything else to wrack your senses, you would still be disgusted by that unpleasant, unbecoming, and preposterous act.

27

Why hurting my senses hurts my mind

It's advisable to be on guard against these disorderly and unsuitable behaviors with as much study, in fact with more, than you gave to that which I've spoken of thus far. It is more difficult to know when one errs in this than in that, since it is obviously easier to hear than to understand. Nevertheless, it often happens that what displeases the senses displeases the intellect as well, but not for the same reasons. As I said earlier, a man should dress according to the custom of others so as not to show that he is reprimanding them or criticizing them. This hurts the feelings of most people who enjoy being admired, but also is offensive to the judgment of reasonable men, for the clothes of another millennium do not fit very well on a person of this one. By the same token those who buy their clothes from a thrift shop are also displeasing, for their doublet clashes with their hose and nothing looks the right size. Many of those things we spoke about before, and perhaps all of them, could be repeated here; they do not observe that decorum we are talking about, neither in itself nor in relation to the time, the place, the person, and the deed, as it should be. The intellect of men appreciates and takes great delight in harmony. But I preferred to gather and arrange my thoughts according to the heading, so to speak, of senses and desires, rather than assign them to the intellect, so that everyone is able to easily recognize them. Everyone experiences feelings and desires quite easily, but not everyone can use their understanding, particularly with that which we call beauty, grace, and charm.

28

Grace, decorum, and restraint—and a special word on fashion sense

Therefore, a man must not be content with doing good things, but he must also study to do them gracefully. Grace is nothing other than that luster which shines from the appropriateness of things that are suitably ordered and well arranged one with the other and together. Without this measure, even the good is not beautiful and beauty is not pleasing. Just as food which, no matter how healthy and nutritious, would not please the guests if it had no flavor or tasted bad, so on occasion it will be with a man's manners. Even if there is nothing harmful in them, they will appear insipid or bitter unless flavored with that certain sweetness called, as I believe, grace or charm. For this reason alone, every vice must be in itself offensive to other people, for vices are such ugly and improper things that their disharmony displeases and perturbs every composed and well-balanced soul. It is most advisable for those who aspire to be pleasant in public dealings to flee vices, especially the dirtier ones such as lust, avarice, cruelty, and the like. Some of these vices are despicable, such as gluttony or drunkenness; some are lewd, such as being a lecher; some are wicked, such as murder. Similarly, other vices are despised by people, some more than others, each for its own nature and quality. But, as I have shown you before, all vices in general, because they are disordered things, render a man unpleasant in the company of others. However, since I undertook to show you men's errors and not their sins, my present care must not be to explore the nature of vice and virtue, but only the proper and improper manners used with others. One of these improper habits was that of Count Ricciardo, whose story I've told you, which was so deformed and dissonant in light of his other beautiful and fitting manners that the worthy bishop immediately noticed it, as a fine and well-trained singer notices wrong notes the instant they are heard. It is therefore suitable for polite people to regard this balance I have spoken about in their walking, standing, sitting, movements, bearing, and in their dress, in their words, in their silence, in their repose, and in their actions. Thus, a man must not embellish himself in the guise of a girl, for his adornments will be one thing, himself another; I see many men who have their hair and beards all curled with a hot iron, and have their faces, necks, and hands so shiny smooth and soft that it would be unsuitable for any young wench, even for a tart more anxious to hawk her wares at a discount than sell them for a decent price. One should smell neither stinky nor sweet, for a gentleman does not smell offensive like a plebeian nor perfumed like a woman or a harlot. Still, I am not saying that at your age you should avoid even certain colognes made from distilled waters. For the reasons I've mentioned above, your clothes should follow the customs of those like you in age and condition. We do not have the power to change customs as we see fit, for it is time that creates them and likewise time consumes them. Everyone, however, may adapt the current fashion to his own personal style. For example, if your legs are very long and the fashion calls for short robes, you could make yours a little less short. If one has very skinny legs, or unusually chubby ones, or perhaps crooked ones, he should not wear hose of loud or garish colors that invite others to admire his defect. None of your outfits should be extremely fancy or overly ornate, such that one can say that you are wearing the stockings of Ganymede or have donned the doublet of Love.[80] But whatever clothes you are sporting, they should suit you and look good, so that it does not appear that you are wearing someone else's. And above all they must conform to your condition, so that a priest does not look like a soldier, or the soldier like a court jester. When Castruccio was in Rome with the Bavarian and enjoyed the glory and pomp of being duke of Lucca and Pistoia, count of Palazzo, a senator of Rome, lord and master at the court of the said Bavarian, he had made, for his pleasure and ostentation, a cloak of crimson velvet which on the breast bore in golden letters a motto, "It is as God wills." And on the back, in similar letters, "It shall be as God wills."[81] I believe you will recognize that this tabard would have been more appropriate for Castruccio's trumpeter than for Castruccio himself. And although kings are above the law, still I could not commend King Manfred for the fact that he always appeared in a green robe.[82] We must therefore take care that clothing fits not only the body but also the status of the one wearing it and, furthermore, is suitable to the place where we live. For as in other countries there are other measures and yet one sells, buys, and trades in every one, so in different localities there are different customs and yet in every land a man may behave and dress himself acceptably. The feathers that Neapolitans and Spaniards pin to their hats, and their fancy ruffles and embroideries, have no place in the wardrobe of serious men or the dress of city dwellers, much less a suit of armor and chain mail. So what is perhaps fashionable in Verona may not do in Venice, for these men, so adorned, so feathered, and armed, are out of place in that venerable city of peace and orderliness. In fact, they appear like nettles and burrs among sweet and edible garden greens, and for this reason are ill received in noble gatherings, because they are so different and odd. A nobleman must not run in the street, nor hurry himself about too much, for this is suitable for the servant and not a gentleman, who will get worn out, sweat and pant for breath, all of which are unbecoming to men of quality. Nor, on the other hand, should one pace stately and demurely as a woman or a bride. Also, it is unsuitable to wobble too much when walking. One should not let his arms dangle, nor swing them backward and forward, nor throw them about so that it looks like he is sowing seed in a field. Nor should you stare a man in the face as if there is something strange in his appearance. There are some who walk like a timorous horse, lifting their legs up high, as if they were pulling their legs out of a bushel basket. Others stomp their feet so forcefully on the ground that they create almost as much noise as a wagon. One man walks pigeon-toed, while another man raises one leg more than the other. There are some men who bend over at every step to pull up their stockings, and some who wiggle their rumps and strut like peacocks. These things are unappealing because, instead of being elegant, they are the opposite. Suppose you have a horse that holds his mouth open or grossly shows his tongue; even though it would not reflect on his real skills, it would affect his price very much and you would get a lot less for him, not because this habit would make him less strong, but because it would be much less graceful. Thus, if one appreciates grace in animals and even in inanimate things, which have no soul or feelings—two solid and comfortable houses will not cost the same if one appears well designed, the other not—how much more should one seek and esteem the graceful in human beings?

29

Bad table manners and getting knee-walking drunk

It is not polite, while at the table, to scratch your head or somewhere else. A man should also, as much as possible, avoid spitting; but if he must, he should do it discreetly. I have often heard it said that there are some nations so sober that their inhabitants today never spit. We could certainly refrain from it for a little while. Nor should one gnaw or chew such that you hear the sound or noises, since there is a difference between the eating of men and pigs. We must also be careful not to gobble up our food and occasion a hiccup or some other unpleasant result, as happens with people who hurry and so gasp for air or breathe so heavily that they annoy their companions. Similarly, it is not proper to clean your teeth with a napkin, nor should you pick at them with a fingernail or a stick or twig, nor should you do this to your ears, for these are hideous acts. Nor is it acceptable to rinse one's mouth with wine and then expectorate in public. And it is not a polite habit to carry a stick in one's mouth when getting up from the table, like a bird making her nest, or to keep it tucked behind the ear like a barber. Those who carry their toothpick tied to chains around their necks are certainly at fault. Besides being a strange tool for a gentleman to be seen taking out of his breast pocket, it reminds us of those instruments for extracting teeth we see standing on dentists' benches. It also shows that person is well equipped and prepared to serve his gluttony, and I don't know why these men don't also carry a spoon tied to the chains around their necks. It is also unsuitable to loll over the table, or to fill both sides of your mouth with food until your cheeks are ready to burst. Also, you must not do anything to proclaim how greatly you are enjoying the food and wine, for this habit is for tavern keepers.[83] To encourage those who are at table with you with words such as "Are you not eating this morning," or "Is there nothing that you like," or "Taste some of this" in my opinion is not laudable, even though the majority of people do it. Though in so doing they show concern for their guest, very often they are also the very reason why he eats so sparingly, for it will seem to him that he is being observed and so he is embarrassed. It is inappropriate, I do believe, to offer something from one's own plate, unless the person who is presenting it is of a much more exalted rank, whereby the person receiving it will consider this an honor. Between men of equal rank, it will seem the person offering somehow or other holds himself superior to the one receiving, and sometimes the guest may not even like to eat what was offered. Not to mention this shows that the banquet does not have sufficient dishes and that they are not evenly distributed, for one person has too much and another not enough, and this could humiliate the lord of the house. Nevertheless, in this matter we must do what is done, and not what should be done, for it is better to blunder with others than be good alone. But whatever the case may be, you must not refuse what is brought to you, as it will seem that you either despise or rebuke the man who has brought it. It is also a barbarous habit to challenge someone to a drinking bout. This is not one of our Italian customs and so we give it a foreign name, that is, *far brindisi*.[84] It has not yet become the practice in our lands and so it should not be done.

If someone should invite you to a drinking contest, you can easily refuse the invitation, saying you give up, thanking him or tasting the wine out of courtesy, without guzzling. Still this toasting with wine, as I have heard several learned men claim, may have been an ancient custom in certain parts of Greece.[85] And they highly praise some man by the name of Socrates who lived at that time because he lasted through an entire night, chugging away with another good man named Aristophanes. The following morning at the break of dawn, he discussed and solved a subtle geometry problem without one mistake, which showed very well that the wine had not bothered him. Learned men further claim that just as risking one's life many times makes a man fearless and sure of himself, so becoming accustomed to the dangers of intemperance makes a man sober and polite. Since drinking wine as a contest in great quantities and to the point of excess in that manner is a great challenge to the strength of the drinker, they claim that it should be done as a test of fortitude and to accustom ourselves to resisting and overcoming the strongest temptations. But notwithstanding this, it seems to me the opposite, and I consider their reasons quite frivolous. We find that learned men, through their grandiose talk, very often manage to allow the wrong side to win and reason to lose, and so we should not trust them in this matter. It could even be that they want to excuse and cover in this fashion the sin of their nation corrupted by this vice, for it could have appeared risky to reprimand others and maybe they feared that they should suffer the same fate as Socrates, who used to go about pointing out everybody's faults. For this reason he was accused out of envy of many heresies and other vile sins, for which he was condemned to death, even though the charges were false and he was, in fact, according to their false idolatries, a good and devout man. It is certain, however, that he does not merit any praise for all the wine he drank that night, for a cask would have drunk, or held, more than he did. And if the wine did not bother him, this was due more to the quality of a robust brain than to the continence of a gentleman. Whatever the ancient chronicles may say about this, I thank blessed God that with all the other plagues that have come to us from across the mountains, this awful one of enjoying inebriation, not only as a game but as a glorious accomplishment, has not yet reached us. Nor am I going to believe that temperance should ever be learned from such teachers as wine and intoxication. The chief steward must not invite strangers, on his own, nor ask them to stay for a meal with his master. No wise man will sit at the table on a servant's invitation. Servants, however, are sometimes so presumptuous that they appropriate their masters' prerogatives. These things are mentioned at this point just in passing, not in following the order established at the outset.

30

The myriad ways to be rude—and an abrupt conclusion

One should not take off his clothes, and especially not his stockings, in public, that is, where decent people would be found; the act is not acceptable in such a place, and it could happen that those body parts which we cover would embarrass him and those who might see them. Do not comb your hair nor wash your hands among other people either, for these are things done in your room, not out in the open. An exception regarding hand washing must be made before sitting down to eat, for then it is reasonable to clean yourself up in the open, even if your hands might not need to be washed, so that anyone who shares from your plate will know for certain. Similarly, one should not go out in public with the coif he wears to bed on his head, nor adjust his clothing in the presence of others. There are some who have the habit of now and then puckering up their lips or screwing up their eyes, or of puffing up their cheeks and blowing out their breath, or of making such similar shifty grimaces. It is best to desist from these habits completely. Once upon a time, the goddess Pallas Athena, according to certain learned men, took great delight in playing a double-reed pipe, and became a genuine master of the instrument.[86] As it happened, one day she was playing for fun near a fountain when she saw her reflection in the water, and seeing the strange contortions of her face, she was embarrassed by them and threw away that double-pipe. In truth she did the right thing, for the cornamuse and crumhorn are no instruments for women, and, in fact, they are equally ill-advised for men, unless the individual be in such dire straits that he must play it professionally and for pay. What I say about unpleasant facial gestures regards, likewise, all the parts of the body. It is not proper either to show one's tongue, or stroke one's beard too much as many have gotten into the habit of doing, or rub your hands together, or sigh, or moan, or twitch, or move in fits and starts, which is what some people do, or stretch out, and while stretching sound off with pleasure, "Oh my! Oh my!" like a yokel waking up in a haystack. Whoever breaks wind with his lips to indicate astonishment or disapproval imitates something gross, and, as you can see, imitations are not far from the real thing. One should not laugh like a buffoon, nor in a boisterous or an insipid way, nor laugh out of habit rather than need. And I do not want you to laugh at your own jokes, for this is a type of self-praise. It is the hearer who should laugh, not the speaker. I do not want to make you believe that since each one of these things represents only a small error, they are, all together, a small error. In fact, out of many little mistakes one big one is made, as I said at the beginning. The smaller they are, the closer others will scrutinize them, for they are not easily perceived, and they sneak into our habits without our noticing them. Just as continual little expenses silently consume our wealth, so these small sins stealthily undermine, with their number and multitude, our distinguished and good behavior. For this reason they are no laughing matter. One should also pay attention to how one moves his body, especially when speaking, for it often happens that one is so concerned with what he is thinking that he does not pay attention to anything else. There are some who shake their heads, who gaze into space, who raise one eyebrow to the middle of their forehead while lowering the other to the chin. They twist up their mouths. They spray spit in the face of whoever is listening. You will also find those who talk with their hands so much it looks like they're catching flies. These are unpleasant tics and rude mannerisms. I once heard it said—I have frequented learned men a lot, as you know—that a worthy man whose name was Pindar used to say that everything that has a sweet and refined taste was flavored by the hand of grace and charm.[87] What must I say about those who leave their study with a pen stuck behind their ears? Or hold their napkins in their teeth? Or rest one of their legs up on the table? Or those who hawk and spit between their feet? Or those who spit on their hands? And what about the infinite other idiotic things people do? One could not list them all—and I am not about to try. Indeed, there may perhaps be many who will think I have already said more than enough.

Notes

1. Joan Wildeblood, *The Polite World: A Guide to Deportment of the English in Former Times* (London: Davis Poynter, 1973), 75.

2. See Spingarn's introduction to his edition of Robert Peterson's 1576 translation *A Renaissance Courtesy-book, Galateo of Manners and Behaviours, by Giovanni Della Casa* (Boston: Merrymount Press, 1914), ix. "One of the two or three treatises of the 1500s that taught good manners to the whole of Europe, and one of the most brilliant examples of the prose of the century," writes Arnaldo Di Benedetto. See Giovanni Della Casa, *Vita di Pietro Bembo*, ed. Antonino Sole (Turin: Fogola, 1997), cover.

3. Giovanni Della Casa, *Vita di Pietro Bembo*, ed. Antonino Sole (Turin: Fogola, 1997), 110.

4. Spingarn, introduction to Peterson, *Renaissance Courtesy-book,* ix.

5. Rudolph M. Bell, *How to Do It: Guides to Good Living for Renaissance Italians* (Chicago: University of Chicago Press, 1999), 282.

6. Anna Bryson, *From Courtesy to Civility: Changing Codes of Conduct in Early Modern England* (Oxford: Clarendon Press, 1998), 77.

7. See *Galateo: A Renaissance Treatise on Manners,* trans. Konrad Eisenbichler and Kenneth R. Bartlett (Toronto: Centre for Reformation and Renaissance Studies, 1994), 9–21.

8. Della Casa to Annibale Rucellai, April 13, 1549, in Emanuela Scarpa, "La biblioteca di Giovanni Della Casa," *La bibliofilia* 82 (1980): 247.

9. *De officiis inter potentiores et tenuiores amicos* (1546), in *Prose di Giovanni Della Casa e altri trattatisti Cinquecenteschi del comportamento*, ed. Arnaldo Di Benedetto (Turin: UTET, 1979) 135–89.

10. Spingarn, introduction to Peterson, *Renaissance Courtesy-book*, xvi.

11. In English, see *Giovanni Della Casa's Poem Book: Ioannis Casae Carminum Liber Florence 1564*, trans. John Van Sickle (Tempe, AZ: Medieval and Renaissance Texts and Studies, 1999). In Italian, *Rime*, ed. Giuliano Tanturli (Milan: Fondazione Pietro Bembo, 2001). Walter L. Bullock, "The Lyric Innovations of Giovanni Della Casa," *PMLA* 41, no. 1 (1926): 82–90; Quinto Marini, "Per una storia della poesia di Giovanni Della Casa," *Italica* 82, nos. 3/4 (2005): 451–71; E. Bonora, "Le Rime di Giovanni Della Casa," in *Retorica e invenzione* (Milan: Rizzoli, 1970), 107–27; and Emanuela Scarpa, *Schede per le Rime di Giovanni Della Casa* (Verona: Fiorini, 2003).

12. See Stephen Miller, *Conversation: A History of a Declining Art* (New Haven: Yale University Press, 2006).

13. Bruce Smith, *Twelfth Night: Texts and Contexts* (New York: Bedford/St. Martin's, 2001). Bruce Smith includes *Galateo* as an important context for Shakespeare's comedy.

14. Claudia Berra, "*Il Galateo* 'fatto per scherzo,'" in *Per Giovanni Della Casa. Ricerche e contributi*, ed. Gennaro Barbarisi and Claudia Berra (Bologna: Cisalpino, 1997), 332.

15. Barbara Bowen, *One Hundred Renaissance Jokes: An Anthology* (Birmingham, AL: Summa, 1988), 3.

16. Della Casa to Piero Vettori, January 29, 1559, quoted in Claudia Berra, "*Il Galateo* 'fatto per scherzo,'" in Per Giovanni Della Casa. Ricerche e contributi, ed. Gennaro Barbarisi and Claudia Berra (Bologna: Cisalpino, 1997), 280.

17. Introduction to *Galateo*, ed. Barbarisi (Venice: Marsilio, 1991), 9–37.

18. *Galateo; or, A Treatise on Politeness and Delicacy of Manners, Addressed to a Young Nobleman from the Italian of Giovanni de la Casa*, trans. Richard Graves (London: J. Dodsley, 1774), ix–xi.

19. From the cover of *Galateo* (Milan: BUR, 2009).

20. See P. M. Forni, *Choosing Civility* (New York: St. Martin's Press, 2002), and *The Civility Solution: What to Do When People Are Rude* (New York: St. Martin's Press, 2008).

GALATEO

The author gratefully acknowledges Randolph Petilos,
Renaldo Migaldi, Susan Tarcov, and all those at the University
of Chicago Press who helped in producing this book.

1. A long explanatory subtitle, in capital letters, was included in the Venice edition of 1558, as well as many later editions: TREATISE OF MISTER GIOVANNI DELLA CASA IN WHICH, UNDER THE PERSONA OF AN IGNORANT OLD MAN, HE INSTRUCTS A YOUNG STUDENT ON WHAT TO DO AND WHAT NOT TO DO IN COMMON CONVERSATION, THUS CALLED GALATEO, OR OF MANNERS. A facsimile of the first separate printed edition (Milan, 1559), which also included this subtitle, has been edited by Giuliano Tanturli (Florence: Polistampa, 2003).

2. The opening phrase, *conciosia cosa, che* in Italian, derives from a standard medieval Latin rhetorical phrase, *cum id sit causa quae*. One of Della Casa's sources, the *Chronicle* of Giovanni Villani (c. 1275–1340), opens the same way, and the author used this phrase in other works. Scholars have traditionally seen this opening as a way the author establishes his persona of the pompous, sometimes forgetful uncle.

3. With the metaphor of life as a journey, Della Casa makes the first of a great many references, more or less accurate, to the *tre corone* (three crowns) of Italian literature, Dante, Petrarch, and Boccaccio. This passage calls to mind the famous opening line of Dante's *Inferno* 1.1: "Nel mezzo del cammin di nostra vita" (Midway in the journey of our life). Petrarch's *Canzoniere*, 37.17–18: "Il tempo passa et l'ore son sì pronte / A fornire il viaggio" (Time flies and every hour is so quick/ to terminate the journey). Quotations from Dante are taken from the translations of Robert Hollander and Jean Hollander, *Inferno* (New York: Doubleday, 2000), *Purgatorio* (2003), and *Paradiso* (2007). Petrarch quotations are from *The Canzoniere, or Rerum vulgarium fragmenta*, trans. Mark Musa (Bloomington: Indiana University Press, 1999).

4. Scholars generally agree that Della Casa was addressing his work to his nephew Annibale Rucellai (d. 1601), who would follow very much his uncle's career, becoming an influential ecclesiastic and ambassador of King Charles IX of France. He also held posts in papal government at Bologna and Ancona and is remembered for edicts against the persecution of the Jews in Rome.

5. Like Machiavelli, Della Casa uses the term "virtù" not in the contemporary ethical sense but rather to mean the skill in accomplishing certain task or role in society.

6. Della Casa's word here, *romitorii,* means hermitages where monks live in seclusion. Throughout the treatise, he develops the contrast between a solitary life of reflection and the active life in society.

7. Here *temperare,* to temper, means more than "to keep under control, to regulate or moderate." It implies the hardening of iron in the forge that renders it superior in strength.

8. Flattery, the use of false compliments to gain personal or political advantage, is a recurring theme in *Galateo.* For an overview of the subject, see Richard Stengel, *You're Too Kind: A Brief History of Flattery*

(New York: Simon & Schuster, 2000). The complex networks of power and the language of targeted adulation are examined in Paul McLean's *The Art of the Network: Strategic Interaction and Patronage in Renaissance Florence* (Durham, NC: Duke University Press, 2007). Della Casa's views here are informed by classical texts, such as Plutarch's "How to Tell a Flatterer from a Friend," *Moralia*, book 4.

9. Here *appetito* has a classical significance familiar to Della Casa from his studies of Aristotle and Cicero. Rather than sensual or sexual desire, it refers to a desire that conforms to one's true nature. Also central throughout *Galateo* is the classical notion of moderation advanced in book 2 of Aristotle's *Nicomachean Ethics*.

10. *Oscitare* (Lat.), which means "to yawn," was used also to signify being lazy and careless. See Cicero, *De oratore* 2.33.144.

11. The translation echoes Robert Peterson's famous phrasing from his translation of 1576: "glare upon your snot." Della Casa parodies a phrase in Petrarch's *Canzoniere* 263.10: "perle et robini et oro."

12. Galateo's *incipit* has given way to a colloquial language resembling that of Boccaccio, ornamented and flavored with Florentine expressions. *Farfalloni* is a Florentine word for catarrh found in Boccaccio's *Corbaccio* (1355). See *The Corbaccio; or, The Labyrinth of Love*, trans. Anthony K. Cassell (Binghamton, NY: Medieval and Renaissance Texts and Studies, 1993).

13. Giovanni Matteo Giberti (1495–1543) of Palermo was a scholar, poet, and the bishop of Verona. Like Della Casa and many other contemporaries mentioned in the treatise, Giberti was devoted to classical literature; he constructed within his palace a printing house devoted to theology and philosophy, especially in Greek.

14. Household here refers to the courtiers and retinue, servants, guests, and friends.

15. Some scholars have argued that the title—in addition to refer-

ring to Galeazzo Florimonte—calls to mind the myth of Galatea, the statue loved by Pygmalion that Aphrodite brings to life. See Ovid's *Metamorphosis* 10.242–97.

16. Italian proverb: "Non fu mai vento senz'acqua."

17. Following Boccaccio again, Della Casa refers to particular fashionable hairstyles, either *tonduti* or *la zazarra*.

18. Ubaldo Bandinelli (1494–1551), Florentine bishop of Montefiascone, was one of the most influential men in Della Casa's life, for whom he wrote the Latin ode *De Ubaldino Bandinelli*. Bandinelli enjoyed fame for his erudition; Bandinelli, Florimonte, and Giberti all lived, as did Della Casa, around the Vatican. See Giovanni Della Casa, *Vita di Pietro Bembo*, trans. Antonio Sole (Turin: Fògola, 1997).

19. Any coin has an intrinsic worth, the value of the metal it is made of, as well as the value it represents symbolically.

20. The first of several specific references to Giovanni Boccaccio's short stories collected in the *Decameron*. *Decameron* 6.4 tells of Chichibio, a cook who serves his wealthy Florentine master a roasted bird with one leg, having already given the other to his mistress. In order to escape punishment, he informs his master that cranes have only one leg. For more on the influence of Boccaccio on *Galateo*, see Ettore Bonora, "Aspetti della prosa del Rinascimento. Il boccaccismo del *Galateo*," *Giornale storico della letteratura italiana* 3 (1956): 349–62; Claudia Berra, "*Il Galateo* 'fatto per scherzo,'" in *Per Giovanni Della Casa. Ricerche e contribuiti*, ed. Gennaro Barbarisi and Claudia Berra (Bologna: Cisalpino, 1997), 271–335; Paola Marconi, "Boccaccio ambiguo maestro di Della Casa. 'Il donare cortesia' nell'episodio de 'Il discreto famigliare' del Galateo," *Italica* 79 (2002): 321–38. Quotations from Boccaccio are from *Decameron*, trans. J. G. Nichols (New York: Alfred A. Knopf, 2008).

21. Following a tradition of misogynist writing, Della Casa com-

posed *An uxor sit ducenda,* a biting commentary on why men should never marry. Two fine Italian translations are available: *Prose di Giovanni Della Casa e altri trattatisti Cinquecenteschi del comportamento,* ed. Arnaldo Di Benedetto (Turin: UTET, 1979), 47–133; *Se s'abbia da prender moglie,* ed. Ugo Enrico Paoli (Florence: Le Monnier, 1946). Boccaccio's *Corbaccio; or, The Labyrinth of Love,* an autobiographical work in the classical tradition, is an important source, both for the colloquial language and for the theme of misogyny.

22. Allusion to Boccaccio, *Decameron* 3.4, the story of Puccio di Rimini, who lived near the convent of San Pancrazio in Florence. He was so pious that he preached the sermons of Frate Nastagio to his wife, "even when she was in a lusty mood."

23. The notion of catharsis in Aristotle, *Poetics* 4.2. See Florindo C. Cerreta, "Alessandro Piccolomini's Commentary on the *Poetics* of Aristotle," *Studies in the Renaissance* 4 (1957): 139–68. For philosophy in the Italian Renaissance, see James Hankins, *Humanism and Platonism in the Italian Renaissance* (Rome: Edizioni di storia e letteratura, 2003), and *The Recovery of Ancient Philosophy in the Renaissance: A Brief Guide* (Florence: L. S. Olschki, 2008).

24. At the end of the third day's stories in the *Decameron,* Filostrato proposes the theme for the next day's tales: "those whose love had an unhappy end."

25. Cecchina is a diminutive of Francesca, while Momo is affectionate for Geronimo.

26. Little is known of Flaminio Tomarozzo, a correspondent of Pietro Bembo and mentioned by Della Casa in *Gaspari Contareni vita.*

27. Dreams are a frequent subject in classical texts: Xenophon, *Cyropaedia* 8.4, and Plato, *Republic* 9.I. See William V. Harris, *Dreams and Experience in Classical Antiquity* (Cambridge: Harvard University Press, 2009).

28. Guccio Imbratta claims to be this titled French aristocrat in Boccaccio, *Decameron* 6.10.

29. Sumptuary laws, restrictions on the sumptuousness of dress, were enacted to curb extravagance, protect fortunes, and make clear distinctions between social classes. For more on fashion and dress codes in the Renaissance, see Alan Hunt, *Governance of the Consuming Passions: A History of Sumptuary Law* (New York: St Martin's Press, 1996); Ann Rosalind Jones and Peter Stallybrass, *Renaissance Clothing and the Materials of Memory*. (New York: Cambridge University Press, 2000); Catherine Kovesi Killerby, *Sumptuary Law in Italy, 1200–1500* (Oxford: Oxford University Press, 2002); Carole Collier Frick, *Dressing Renaissance Florence: Families, Fortunes, and Fine Clothing* (Baltimore: John Hopkins University Press, 2002); Ulinka Rublack, *Dressing Up: Cultural Identity in Renaissance Europe* (Oxford: Oxford University Press, 2010); Roberta Orsi Landini, *Moda a Firenze, 1540–1580* (Florence: Pagliai, 2011).

30. Giotto (1264–1337) was the greatest Italian painter and architect of the fourteenth century, architect of the bell tower of Florence Cathedral. Giotto's family was originally from Vicchio in Mugello, not Della Casa's family home in Borgo San Lorenzo.

31. The term *cerimonie* has for Della Casa a pejorative meaning and signifies any empty compliment or excessive, fatuous ritual and formality. There was much discussion about and satire on the titles and formalities imported into Italy from Spain. For the influence of Spain on Italy, see Benedetto Croce, "Le cerimonie spagnuole in Italia" in *La Spagna nella vita italiana durante la Rinascenza* (Bari: Laterza, 1917), 172–96.

32. The connection between violence and honor, and the "culture of knives," are brilliantly presented by Giancarlo Baronti in his *Coltelli d'Italia. Rituali di violenza e tradizione produttive nel mondo popolare*

(Padua: Muzzio Editore, 1986). See Giovanni Battista Possevino, *Dialogo dell'honore* (Venice, 1553).

33. Della Casa here ponders the formal/informal registers of address in the Italian language, which distinguishes between the *tu* and the *Lei* forms. Della Casa is preoccupied with the subtle operation of establishing boundaries and an appropriate degree of distance or familiarity. These distinctions tend to be lost in English today, although it might help to consider the use of professional titles and the choice of being on a first- or last-name basis.

34. Boccaccio, *Decameron* 5.6. Ruggiero di Lauria (c.1250–1305) was an admiral of the Aragonese fleet. Frederick II (1272–1337) was king of Sicily from 1295 until his death.

35. Here the theme of flattery reappears, focused on greetings and salutations. The modern reader might recoil from "I am your slave" but should be reminded that the "ciao" derives from "schiavo," your slave. Formal valedictions, such as "I have the honour to be Your Majesty's humble and obedient servant," are still officially observed when writing to English royalty.

36. Latin salutation: "Si tu vales, bene est; ego valeo."

37. The Greek poet is almost surely Euripides (c. 480–406 BC), although the particular reference is here, as elsewhere, imprecise.

38. Sophocles, *Oedipus at Colonus*, vv. 1143–44. Translation by Robert Fagles in Sophocles, *The Three Theban Plays* (New York: Penguin, 1984).

39. John Duns Scotus (1266–1308), one of the most important medieval philosophers and theologians, was known as "the Subtle Doctor."

40. Boccaccio, *Decameron* 6.5. Forese da Rabatta, riding with Giotto through muddy terrain, makes fun of the painter for looking so ugly yet being capable of such beauty.

41. Terence, *The Brothers* 4.5.696–97: "Why don't I tease him a lit-

tle?" This comedy by the Roman playwright, a writer Della Casa knew very well, explores the theme of raising children. Translation by Peter Brown, *The Comedies of Terence* (Oxford: Oxford University Press, 2010).

42. Boccaccio, *Decameron* 9.8. Ciacco, in revenge for a trick played on him by Biondello, sends Filippo an offensive message signed by Biondello. For this, Filippo beats up Biondello in the Loggia degli Adimari Cavicciuli, which stood at the corner of Via delle Oche in Florence.

43. Boccaccio, *Decameron* 6.7. Filippa da Prato is accused of infidelity but answers that she did not wish to waste her husband's leftovers.

44. There is a play on words here: *lupo* is the Italian word for wolf and the first name of a member of a wealthy and powerful Florentine family, the Uberti. This passage is taken from Giovanni Villani's *Chronicle* 7.119–20.

45. This passage is taken almost verbatim from Boccaccio, *Decameron* 6.3.

46. *Decameron* 6.1. The knight began to tell Oretta a story, but he expressed himself so poorly that she asked him to stop.

47. "Et: Gli fece ungner le mani con la grassa di S. Gio Boccadoro": an image of Saint John was stamped on a Florentine coin; thus "he is corrupted by the grease of the saint." "Dove mi manda egli." "Ad Arno": this witticism appears in *Decameron* 6.2. A fourth one in the original goes like this: "Va chiama il Barbieri." "Et perché non il Barbadomani." The Italian word *barbieri* ends with the same letters as the word for yesterday, *ieri*, while *domani* is the word for tomorrow. Richard Graves, in his fine version of *Galateo* (1774), added his own bad jokes: "Where is my Lord? In his clothes, unless he is in the bathroom or in bed"; "How does this wine taste? A little moist, I think"; "How is this dish to be eaten? With your mouth" (113). The witticisms Della Casa quotes are similar.

48. The bawdy narrator in Boccaccio's *Decameron* 5.10.

49. See Castiglione's *Book of the Courtier*, book 2. For more on the

subject, see Robert Grudin, "Renaissance Laughter: The Jests in Castiglione's *Il Cortigiano*," *Neophilologus* 58 (1979): 199–204; Barbara Bowen, *One Hundred Renaissance Jokes: An Anthology* (Birmingham, AL: Summa, 1988) and *Humour and Humanism in the Renaissance* (Burlington, VT: Ashgate/Variorum, 2004). For a classical source, see Cicero, *De oratore* 2.54–70.

50. From Dioneo's obscene song in *Decameron* 5, conclusion: "Madonna Aldruda, levate la coda, che buone novelle vi reco."

51. Via del Cocomero is today Via Ricasoli. The Basilica of San Lorenzo, in the parish of the Rucellai, was designed under the supervision of Filippo Brunelleschi (1377–1446). Leo X commissioned Michelangelo to construct a façade in 1518, but it was never completed.

52. Dante, *Inferno* 1.68–69: "e li parenti miei furon lombardi / mantoani per patria ambedui."

53. Cremona was an important city in Lombardy, while Gazzuolo was an ordinary village near Mantua.

54. *Decameron* 1.8. Erminio Grimaldi was known by the nickname Erminio Avarizia.

55. Petrarch, *Canzoniere* 366.76–78: "Ricorditi che fece il peccar nostro / prender Dio per scamparne / umana carne al tuo virginal chiostro."

56. Giovanni Villani, *Chronicle* 9.136.

57. Richard Graves put these Italian words into similarly antique English ones: welkin, guerdon, lore, meed, eftsoons (124).

58. Antonio Alamanni (1464–1528), *Sonetto alla Burchiellesca*: "Io vidi un che da sette passatoi / Fu da un canto all'altro trapassato."

59. Dante, *Inferno* 23.101–2: "che li pesi / fan così cigolar le lor bilance." And 17.85–86: " 'l riprezzo / de la quartana."

60. Dante, *Inferno* 22.25–26: "a l'orlo de l'acqua d'un fosso / stanno i ranocchi pur col muso fuori."

61. Dante, *Inferno* 28.22. "Già veggia, per mezzul perdere o lulla?"

62. Master Brufaldo, unidentified, was perhaps a Florentine fool or buffoon.

63. *Rinculare* is a verb meaning to move backward, formed from the word for "ass," *culo*.

64. Dante, *Inferno* 25.2: "Le mani alzò con amendue le fiche." *Fiche* is slang for the female genitals. The gesture of thumb between index and middle finger is synonymous with the middle finger. Women use the euphemism "chestnuts."

65. Dante, *Inferno* 17.117: "se non che al viso e di sotto mi venta."

66. Dante, *Purgatorio* 18.111 and 113–14: "però ne dite ond'è presso i pertugio" and "e un di quelli spirti disse: Vieni / di retro a noi, e troverai la buca."

67. Dante, *Inferno* 18.133: "Taïde è, la puttana."

68. Boccaccio, *Decameron* 1.2. Before going to bed with her village priest, Belcolor accepts his gift of a fine cloak of Turkish cloth.

69. Dante, *Purgatorio* 30.142–45: "Alto fato di Dio sarebbe rotto / se Letè si passasse e tal vivanda / fosse gustata sanza alcuno scotto / di pentimento che lagrime spanda."

70. Dante, *Paradiso* 12.55–56. "dentro vi nacque l'amoroso drudo / de la fede cristiana."

71. Dante, *Paradiso* 17.129: "e lascia pur grattar dov' è la rogna."

72. Boccaccio, *Decameron* 4.3.

73. Dante, *Purgatorio* 30.131: "imagini di ben seguendo false."

74. Petrarch, *Canzoniere* 210.14: "del fiorir queste inanzi tempo tempie."

75. Dante, *Inferno* 4.141: "Tulïo e Lino e Seneca morale." Della Casa objects to the Greek mythological figure of Linus being included with Cicero and Seneca.

76. From the sonnet "Io vidi un dí spogliar tutte in farsetto" by

the Florentine barber-poet Burchiello (1404–49): "l'uno era padovano e l'altro laico" (12).

77. Polyclitus, whose name means "very clear," was the most celebrated sculptor in ancient Greece (450–420 BC).

78. Theodorus was a noted actor in antiquity, remembered also by Castiglione in book 2 of *The Courtier*. Della Casa's source is probably Aristotle's *Politics* 7.15.10.

79. Zeuxis of Heraclea (d. 397 BC), mythic Greek painter.

80. In Greek mythology, Ganymede is a divine hero whose homeland was Troy. Homer describes Ganymede as the most beautiful of mortals.

81. Castruccio Castracani (1281–1328), was duke of Lucca. See Machiavelli's *Vita di Castruccio Castracani* (1520) and Villani's *Chronicle* 10.60.

82. Manfred (1232–66), the son of Federico II, became king of the Two Sicilies. He died battling Carlo d'Angio.

83. In the printed version, the name Cinciglion, a character from Boccaccio, *Decameron* 1.6, is used for drunkards.

84. The Italian word for "to toast" comes from German *ich bring dir's*, "I bring it to you."

85. In ancient Greece, the symposium was a drinking party. Literary works that describe or take place at a symposium include Plato's *Symposium* and Xenophon's *Symposium*. See Andrew Dalby, *Siren Feasts: A History of Food and Gastronomy in Greece* (New York: Routledge, 1996); Peter Garnsey, *Food and Society in Classical Antiquity* (Cambridge: Cambridge University Press, 1999). For the Italian Renaissance context, see John Varriano, *Food and Art in Renaissance Italy* (Berkeley: University of California Press, 2009).

86. Plutarch, *Life of Alcibiades* 2: "During his school days, he was generally quite good at obeying his teachers, but he refused to learn the pipes on the grounds that it was not appropriate for a person of

noble and free birth. He argued that there was no disfigurement and distortion of the appearance proper to a free man in wielding a plectrum and playing the lyre, but that when a person set pipes to his mouth and started to blow even his close friends would find it pretty difficult to recognize his features. Besides, he said, the lyre can accompany the voice and singing of its player, whereas the pipes muzzle and obstruct a person and rob him of his ability to express himself in words." *Greek Lives*, trans. Robin Waterfield (Oxford: Oxford World Classics, 1998).

87. Pindar (522–442 BC) was a Greek lyric poet. See *Olympian* 1.30–33: "Grace, who brings to fulfillment all things for men's delight, / Bestowing favor, many times makes / Things incredible seem true." *The Odes of Pindar*, trans. Richard Lattimore (Chicago: University of Chicago Press, 1959).

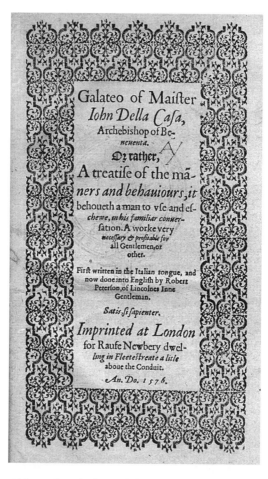

Galateo of Maiſter
Iohn Della Caſa,
Archebiſhop of Be-
neuenta.

Oꝛ rather,
A treatiſe of the mā-
ners and behauiours, it
behoueth a man to vſe and eſ-
chewe, in his familiar conuer-
ſation. A worke very
neceſſary & profitable for
all Gentlemen, or
other.

Firſt written in the Italian tongue, and
now done into Engliſh by Robert
Peterſon, of Lincolnes Inne
Gentleman.

Satis ſi ſapienter.

Imprinted at London
for Raufe Newbery dwel-
ling in Fleeteſtreate a litle
aboue the Conduit.

An. Do. 1 5 7 6.

Title page from the first English translation of *Galateo* (1576).
By permission of the Folger Shakespeare Library.

Bibliography

Galateo appeared in print for the first time in the *Rime et prose di M. Giovanni della Casa* (Venice: Nicolò Bevilacqua, 1558). The first separate edition appeared the following year: *Il Galateo, di M. Giovanni della Casa; ovvero Trattato de' Costumi* (Milan: Antonio degli Antonii, 1559). *Opere di Monsig. Giovanni Della Casa* (Florence: Appresso Giuseppe Marini, 1707) was the first of several complete works in the eighteenth century. It was followed by *Opere di Monsignor Giovanni della Casa* (Venice: Angiolo Pasinelli, 1728–29), a second edition in 1752, and a Naples edition in 1733.

The standard bibliography remains Antonio Santosuosso's *The Bibliography of Giovanni Della Casa: Books, Readers and Critics, 1537–1975* (Florence: Olschki, 1979). The extensive secondary material on *Galateo* in Italian is recorded in Stefano Prandi, ed., *Galateo* (Turin: Einaudi, 2000), lii–lix. Of bibliographic interest is Emanuela Scarpa's "La biblioteca di Giovanni della Casa," *La bibliofilia* 82 (1980): 247–80.

The textual history and problems of *Galateo* are discussed in Gennaro Barbarisi, *Galateo* (Venice: Marsilio, 1991), 9–40, and Prandi, xl–xlv, as well as other recent Italian editions. See Emanuela Scarpa, "Appunti per l'edizione critica del 'Galateo,'" *Filologia e critica* 6 (1981): 189–258, and "Schede sulle recenti fortune del 'Galateo' di Giovanni della Casa (con un'appendice gualteruzziana)," *Filologia e critica* 22 (1997): 37–75. Also useful is Gennaro Barbarisi, "Ancora sul testo del 'Galateo,'" in *Per Giovanni Della Casa. Ricerche e contributi* (Milan: Cisalpino, 1997), 253–70.

For the history of *Galateo* and conduct books in English, see M. P. Tilley, "Della Casa's *Galateo* in Seventeenth-Century England," *Romantic Review* 9 (1918): 309–12; Hilary Adams, *Il Cortigiano* and *Il Galateo*, *Modern Language Review* 42 (1947): 457–66; R. S. Pine-Coffin, "A Note on Books of Courtesy in England," in *Galateo or The Book of Manners* (Harmondsworth, Middlesex: Penguin, 1958), 105–31; John Woodhouse, "The Tradition of Della Casa's *Galateo* in English," in *The Crisis of Courtesy*, ed. Jacques Carré (New York: E. J. Brill, 1994), 11–26; and Peter Burke, *The Fortunes of the Courtier: The European Reception of Castiglione's Cortigiano* (State College: Pennsylvania State University Press, 1996).

Galateo of Maister Iohn Della Casa, Archebishop of Beneuenta. Trans. Robert Peterson. London: Raufe Newbery, 1576.

The Refin'd Courtier; or, A Correction of Several Indecencies Crept into Civil Conversation. Trans. Nathaniel Walker. London: Printed by J. G. for R. Royston, 1663.

Casa his Galateus; or, A Treatise on Manners: Wherein a Father Instructs his Son how to Carry Himself so as to Gain the Character of a Well-bred and Accomplisht Gentleman. Trans. William Hustler, John Hals, et. al. London: William Davis, [1701].

Galateo; or, A Treatise on Politeness and Delicacy of Manners, Addressed to a Young Nobleman from the Italian of Giovanni de la Casa. Trans. Richard Graves. London: J. Dodsley, 1774.

Galateo or the Book of Manners. Trans. R. S. Pine-Coffin. Harmondsworth, Middlesex: Penguin, 1958.

Galateo: A Renaissance Treatise on Manners. Translated with an introduction and notes by Konrad Eisenbichler and Kenneth R. Bartlett. Toronto: Centre for Reformation and Renaissance Studies, 1994.

At least one new critical edition of *Galateo* was published in each decade of the twentieth century (see Prandi, lii). Introductions and notes to these editions are valuable.

Galateo. With an introduction by Carlo Steiner. Milan: Vallardi, 1910.

Galateo. With an introduction and notes by Ugo Scoti-Bertinelli. Turin: Paravia, 1921.

Galateo: ovvero De' Costumi. Ed. Pietro Pancrazi. Florence: Le Monnier, 1940.

Galateo, ovvero de' costumi. Ed. Bruno Maier. Milan: Mursia, 1971.

Il Galateo. In *Prose di Giovanni Della Casa e altri trattatisti cinquecenteschi del comportamento*, ed. Arnaldo Di Benedetto, 191–263. Turin: UTET, 1979.

Galateo. Ed. Gennaro Barbarisi. Venice: Marsilio, 1991.

Galateo. Ed. Stefano Prandi. Introduction by Carlo Ossola. Turin: Einaudi, 2000.

Galateo. Ed. Claudio Milanini. Introduction by Giorgio Manganelli. Milan: BUR, 2009.

Galateo. Ed. Saverio Orlando. Milan: Garzanti, 2011.

ON GIOVANNI DELLA CASA AND *GALATEO*

Three excellent collections of essays cover the wide range of Della Casa's life and writing: Gennaro Barbarisi and Claudia Berra, eds., *Per Giovanni Della Casa. Ricerche e contributi* (Bologna: Cisalpino, 1997); Stefano Carrai. *Giovanni Della Casa, ecclesiastico e scrittore* (Rome: Edizioni di storia e letteratura, 2007); Amedeo Quondam, *Giovanni Della Casa. Un seminario per il centenario* (Rome: Bulzoni, 2006).

Binni, Walter. "Giovanni Della Casa." In *Critici e poeti dal Cinquecento al Novecento*, 17–31. Florence: La Nuova Italia, 1951.

Bell, Rudolph M. *How to Do It: Guides to Good Living for Renaissance Italians*. Chicago: University of Chicago Press, 1999.

Berger, Harry. *The Absence of Grace: Sprezzatura and Suspicion in Two Renaissance Courtesy Books*. Stanford, CA: Stanford University Press, 2000.

Berra, Claudia. "*Il Galateo* 'Fatto per scherzo.'" In *Per Giovanni Della Casa. Ricerche e contribuiti*, ed. Gennaro Barbarisi and Claudia Berra, 271–335. Bologna: Cisalpino, 1997.

Biow, Douglas. *The Culture of Cleanliness in Renaissance Italy*. New York: Cornell University Press, 2006.

———. *In Your Face: Professional Improprieties and the Art of Being Conspicuous in Sixteenth-Century Italy*. Stanford, CA: Stanford University Press, 2010.

Bonora, Ettore. "Aspetti della prosa del Rinascimento. Il boccaccismo del '*Galateo*.'" *Giornale storico della letteratura italiana* 3 (1956): 349–62.

Bryson, Anna. *From Courtesy to Civility: Changing Codes of Conduct in Early Modern England*. Oxford: Clarendon Press, 1998.

Burke, Peter. "The Language of Gesture in Early Modern Italy." In *A Cultural History of Gesture*, ed. J. Bremmer and H. Roodenburg, 71–83. Cambridge, MA: B. Blackwell, 1991.

Caretti, Lanfranco. "Della Casa, uomo pubblico e scrittore." In *Antichi e moderni. Studi di letteratura italiana*,135–50. Turin: Einaudi, 1976.

Cowan, Alexander. *Marriage, Manners and Mobility in Early Modern Venice*. Burlington, VT: Ashgate, 2007,

Cox, Virginia. *The Renaissance Dialogue: Literary Dialogue in Its Social and Political Contexts. Castiglione to Galileo*. Cambridge: Cambridge University Press, 1992.

Crane, Thomas Frederick. *Italian Social Customs of the Sixteenth Century, and Their Influence on the Literatures of Europe.* New Haven: Yale University Press, 1920.

Di Benedetto, Arnaldo. "Giovanni Della Casa e il *Galateo.*" In *Stile e linguaggio,* 78–85. Rome, 1974.

———. "Ironia e piacevolezza nel *Galateo.*" *Critica letteraria* 31 (1981): 245–51.

Elias, Norbert. *The Civilizing Process: Sociogenetic and Psychogenetic Investigations.* Trans. Edmund Jephcott. Oxford: Blackwell, 2000.

Falvo, Giuseppe. "Il *Galateo* e le *Rime* di Giovanni Della Casa." *Italian Culture* 9 (1991): 129–38.

Greenblatt, Stephen. *Renaissance Self-Fashioning: From More to Shakespeare.* Chicago: University of Chicago Press, 1983.

Griggio, Claudio. "Tradizione e rinnovamento nella cultura del *Galateo.*" *Lettere italiane* 26 (1974): 415–33.

Horodowich, Elizabeth. *Language and Statecraft in Early Modern Venice.* New York: Cambridge University Press, 2008.

Javitch, Daniel. *Poetry and Courtliness in Renaissance England.* Princeton, NJ: Princeton University Press. 1978.

Kolsky, Stephen. *Courts and Courtiers in Renaissance Northern Italy.* Burlington, VT: Ashgate/Variorum, 2003.

Lawrence, Jason. *"Who the Devil Taught Thee So Much Italian?": Italian Language Learning and Literary Imitation in Early Modern England.* New York: Palgrave, 2005.

Lievsay, John. *Stefano Guazzo and the English Renaissance, 1575–1675.* Chapel Hill: University of North Carolina Press, 1961.

Marconi, Paola. "Boccaccio ambiguo maestro di Della Casa. 'Il donare cortesia' nell'episodio de 'Il discreto famigliare' del Galateo." *Italica* 79 (2002): 321–38.

Montanari, Massimo. *L'Europa a tavola. Storia dell'alimentazione dal Medioevo ad oggi.* Rome-Bari: Laterza, 2004.

Morgana, Silvia. "La lingua del *Galateo*." In *Per Giovanni Della Casa. Ricerche e contributi*, ed. Gennaro Barbarisi and Claudia Berra, 337–69. Milan: Cisalpino, 1997.

Olivieri, Mario. *Costumato, piacevole e di bella maniera. Della Casa, Castiglione, Guazzo: la civiltà come conversazione*. Rome: Bulzoni, 2008.

Panichi, Nicola. *La virtù eloquente. La "civil conversazione" nel Rinascimento*. Urbino: Editrice Montefeltro, 1994.

Patrizi, Giorgio. *Galateo* di Giovanni Della Casa." In *Letteratura italiana. Le opere*, vol. 2, Turin: Einaudi, 1993.

Pirotti, Umberto. "Il Della Casa del *Galateo*." *Studi e problemi di critica testuale* 10 (1975): 29–56.

Prosperi, Gianluca. "Per una lettura antropologica del *Galateo* di Della Casa." *Studium* 3 (1980): 379–86.

Quondam, Amedeo. *La conversazione. Un modello italiano*. Rome: Donzelli, 2007.

———. *Forma del vivere. L'etica del gentiluomo e i moralisti italiani*. Bologna: Il Mulino, 2011.

Rebhorn, Wayne A. *Courtly Performances: Masking and Festivity in Castiglione's Book of the Courtier*. Detroit: Wayne State University Press, 1978.

Richards, Jennifer. *Rhetoric and Courtliness in Early Modern Literature*. Cambridge: Cambridge University Press, 2003.

Romagnoli, Daniela. "Parlare a tempo e luogo. Galatei prima del *Galateo*." In *Educare il copo, educare la parola. Nella trattatistica del Rinascimento*. Ed. Giorgio Patrizi and Amedeo Quondam. Rome: Bulzoni, 1998.

Saccone, Eduardo. *Le buone e le cattive maniere. Letteratura e galateo nel Cinquecento*. Bologna: Il Mulino, 1992.

Santoro, Marco. "La "discrezione" nel *Galateo* di Giovanni Della Casa." In *Fortuna, ragione e prudenza nella civiltà letteraria del Cinquecento*, 545–82. Naples: Liguori, 1978.

Santosuosso, Antonio. "Giovanni Della Casa and His *Galateo*: On Life and Success in the Late Italian Renaissance." *Renaissance and Reformation* 11 (1975): 1–13.

———. *Vita di Giovanni Della Casa*. Rome: Bulzoni, 1978.

Scaglione, Aldo. *Knights at Court: Courtliness, Chivalry, and Courtesy from Ottonian Germany to the Italian Renaissance*. Berkeley: University of California Press, 1991.

Scarpati, Claudio. "Il Sistema del *Galateo*." In *Invenzione e scrittura. Saggi di letteratura italiani*, 163–76. Milan: Vita e pensiero, 2005.

Sole, Antonino. *Cognizione del reale e letteratura in Giovanni Della Casa*. Rome: Bulzoni, 1981.

Von Boehn, Max. *Modes and Manners: The Sixteenth Century*. Trans. Joan Joshua. London: George G. Harrap, 1932.

Wildeblood, Joan. *The Polite World: A Guide to the Deportment of the English in Former Times*. London: Davis-Poynter, 1973.

Wyatt, Michael. *The Italian Encounter with Tudor England: A Cultural Politics of Translation*. New York: Cambridge University Press, 2005.